A STUDENT'S GUIDE TO
INTERNATIONAL RELATIONS

THE PRESTON A. WELLS JR.
GUIDES TO THE MAJOR DISCIPLINES

⛄

PHILOSOPHY *Ralph M. McInerny*

LITERATURE *R. V. Young*

LIBERAL LEARNING *James V. Schall, S.J.*

THE STUDY OF HISTORY *John Lukacs*

THE CORE CURRICULUM *Mark C. Henrie*

U.S. HISTORY *Wilfred M. McClay*

ECONOMICS *Paul Heyne*

POLITICAL PHILOSOPHY *Harvey C. Mansfield*

PSYCHOLOGY *Daniel N. Robinson*

CLASSICS *Bruce S. Thornton*

AMERICAN POLITICAL THOUGHT *George W. Carey*

RELIGIOUS STUDIES *D. G. Hart*

THE STUDY OF LAW *Gerard V. Bradley*

NATURAL SCIENCE *Stephen M. Barr*

MUSIC HISTORY *R. J. Stove*

A Student's Guide to International Relations

Angelo M. Codevilla

WILMINGTON, DELAWARE

A Student's Guide to International Relations is made possible by grants from the Lee and Ramona Bass Foundation, the Huston Foundation, the Lillian S. Wells Foundation, the Barre Seid Foundation, and the Grover Hermann Foundation. The Intercollegiate Studies Institute gratefully acknowledges their support.

Copyright © 2010 by Angelo M. Codevilla

Codevilla, Angelo, 1943–
    A student's guide to international relations / Angelo M. Codevilla.
    p. cm. —(Student guides to the major disciplines)
    ISBN 978-1-935191-91-9

       1. International relations. I. Title.

JZ1242.C632 2010
327—dc22   2010020118

ISI Books
3901 Centerville Road
Wilmington, DE 19807-1938
www.isibooks.org

Design by Sam Torode
Manufactured in the United States of America

CONTENTS

❧

INTRODUCTION

⁂

The number of students majoring in international relations (IR) today dwarfs that of a generation ago. But whereas a student who majors in mathematics or even economics can expect a more or less uniform curriculum regardless of the university or the professor, students of IR will find the field defined differently at different institutions and by different professors. This guide points the student toward what is essential in the field and to the books most likely to help one make sense of a complex world.

What Is IR?

The art by which governments and peoples deal with one another goes by many names: diplomacy, statecraft, foreign affairs, foreign relations. Formal education does not define this art. Rather, statesmen have defined it by practicing it. Whoever practices it successfully must have in mind an accurate picture of his own country's character, needs, objectives, and capacities, as well as those of foreign countries. Knowledge of the techniques of international intercourse is helpful. The history of past events also illuminates current choices. These things can be learned from books to a considerable extent.

In American higher education, IR is a term that covers courses in "American foreign policy," "area studies," "IR theory," "international institutions," "peace studies," "conflict resolution," and "game theory," as well as courses in what was once the whole field, namely, "diplomatic history." Such courses may be offered by political science departments (IR is one of political science's four traditional subdisciplines), by departments of IR, or in any of the thirty-five professional schools of international affairs, such as Tufts University's Fletcher School of Law and Diplomacy or John Hopkins's School of Advanced International Studies. Students may reach the Ph.D. via any of these paths.

Students typically focus on one or more of IR's many aspects, such as U.S. foreign policy or the study of a specific region, and they usually combine IR with another field, such as economics or even public health. Many are simply interested in learning what lies behind the headlines about the big events on the international scene.

These events are well worth understanding because nations are born and die through relations with one another. The United States' independence became possible because of a complex struggle between Britain, France, and Spain. Greek, rather than Persian, civilization is our heritage because the Athenians defeated King Xerxes' navy at Salamis in 480 B.C. Our civilization is Christian rather than Islamic because Charles Martel marshaled Frankish tribes to stop the Muslim invasion of Europe at the Battle of Tours in A.D. 732. The history of international affairs is the record of peoples who have shown the best and the worst of which human beings are capable. As Charles Hill illustrates in *Grand Strategies: Literature, Statecraft, and World Order* (2010), international affairs has been the subject of some of the world's great literature.

American authors and teachers today tend to reflect the schools of thought about foreign affairs that have developed here since the early twentieth century in the course of American political struggles. These schools differ radically from how Americans approached the world from the Founding until circa 1900, as well as from how foreign affairs have classically been taught.

New America, Old World

America's Founders drew their guidance in international affairs from history's store of wisdom and folly. Plutarch's *Lives* was Alexander Hamilton's favorite authority. In Latin and Greek, the Founders absorbed Thucydides' account of classical Greece's self-destructive diplomacy, Livy's tale of Rome's rise through conquest, and Tacitus's account of the early emperors' attempts to rule the known world. Most had read Machiavelli, and all were avid followers of the struggles between Europe's eighteenth-century sovereigns. Remarkably, the Founders agreed that America's relations with the rest of the world should bear as little resemblance as possible to those of Athens, Sparta, Rome, Paris, or London. As heirs to the British Whig tradition expressed in Viscount Bolingbroke's *Patriot King* (1738), and in accord with the new understanding of economics being elaborated by the French Encyclopedist Turgot (1750) and the Scottish moral philosopher Adam Smith (1776), they believed that the statesman's primary duty was to avoid needless war. Their proximate objective was to minimize foreign interference in the American people's unique character and independent development.

George Washington's 1796 Farewell Address had encapsulated their generation's foreign policy. Secretary of State John Quincy Adams, in his July 4, 1821, address to the U.S. House of Representatives as well as in the documents associated with the Monroe Doctrine of 1823, explained the policy: Peaceful commerce with all nations, and good wishes to all regardless of their governance or culture. To avoid foreign interference in our affairs, Americans would mind their own domestic business. In Adams's words, America "goes not abroad in search of monsters to destroy. She is the well-wisher to the freedom and independence of all," but "the champion and vindicator only of her own." Bordering states, nearby islands, and then the oceans would concern America— in that order. The rest of the world would matter insofar as it affected these. What is nearest is dearest.

The U.S. government neither could nor would interfere with Americans pouring into the nearly empty lands between the Mississippi and the Pacific. When this flood of settlers brought war with Mexico, some Americans wanted the U.S. government to take more than that country's empty lands, while others, including Adams, objected to allowing even the independent Texans to join the union, in part because they feared it would compromise America's domestic character and bring war between the union's slave and free states. During and after the Civil War (1861–65), American foreign policy was under the direction of Abraham Lincoln's secretary of state, William Seward, who pursued Adams's vision of America's greatness by rolling back France's claims on Mexico and Britain's claims on any canal that might be dug across central America, as well as by encouraging immigration and peaceful expansion (e.g., the Alaska purchase, 1867). The next major figure in U.S. foreign policy, Secretary of State James G. Blaine (1881, 1889–92), did his best to follow in Seward's and Adams's footsteps. Not until the Spanish-American War of 1898 did any major American figure suggest that the Founders' pursuit of the national interest through mutual noninterference might be flawed.

On the surface, the main division in U.S. foreign policy after the Spanish-American War was between those who, like Senator Albert Beveridge, wanted America to become a colonial power and those who, like Andrew Carnegie, did not. By 1905 the disagreement had become irrelevant, because experience in the Philippines had extinguished appetite for conquest.

The more important question was, to what end should America's new power be exercised? A fundamental division had been widening since the 1880s, and it continues with us today. On one side were (and are) those who conflate America's interests with mankind's. They rejected the Founders' view that American statesmen must act almost exclusively in the American people's interests, that relations with other nations must be at arm's length, and that America must ask no more of foreign nations than it is willing and able to enforce by war. On the other side were those such as Theodore Roosevelt, who, while delighted to expand America's influence, kept the Founders' focus on America's peculiar national interests and always measured ends sought by means available. For example, because Roosevelt believed that each of the world's peoples guarded its own interests jealously, his mediation of the Russo-Japanese War of 1905 did not commit the United States to any particular outcome or proposal.

Today's Three Schools

At the turn of the twentieth century, some Americans began to think of themselves as mankind's benefactors, teachers, and leaders. They argued that the Founders' concentration on America's interests, and the limitation of their demands on other nations to what America could expect to enforce, concurred with an international order of selfishness and war. Stanford University's founding president, David Starr Jordan (*World Peace and the College Man,* 1916; *Ways to Lasting Peace,* 1916), and Columbia University's president, Nicholas Murray Butler (*The International Mind: An Argument for the Judicial Settlement of International Disputes,* 1912), were among the prominent liberal Americans who regarded themselves as "internationalists"—that is, they were concerned with mankind's common interest rather than just with America's. They derogated those who looked at international affairs from the perspective of their country's particular interest as "isolationists."

Woodrow Wilson's presidential speeches (1913–21) provide an enduring summary of the views of liberal internationalism: America is destined to lead the world to the peace and democracy that all mankind supposedly desires, by intervening in quarrels in and between foreign nations, by fostering modernization, by transferring power from nations to international institutions, and by exemplary disarmament. Because liberal internationalists believe that all peoples ultimately want the same things, they are more concerned with pushing events toward desired ends than with what the means they use will actually produce. Hence, though they often choose military measures, they reject war in the dictionary sense of the word. For example, when Woodrow Wilson led America into World War I, he took pains to argue that America would make this a war like no other—not for anyone's advantage but for mankind's. According to Wilson, it was to be "the war that ends all wars."

From this trunk the other dominant schools of contemporary American statecraft have branched. During the 1920s and 1930s, this liberal internationalist trunk consisted of America's political elite, including President Herbert Hoover and such "isolationists" as Senators Gerald Nye (R-ND) and William Borah (R-ID). All were ardent supporters of the Kellogg-Briand Pact, which outlawed war (and committed America to punish violators of the pact). Borah famously accused Robert Lansing, who had been Wilson's secretary of state, of warmongering because Lansing opposed the treaty's ratification. The ranks of liberal internationalists also included America's elite in business and law: Thomas Watson Sr. of IBM, Thomas Lamont of J. P. Morgan, Bernard Baruch, and Henry Morgenthau. Their number included attorney John Foster Dulles of Sullivan and Cromwell, America's most prominent Protestant layman, who had been Wilson's student at Princeton and became President Dwight Eisenhower's secretary of state. President Franklin D. Roosevelt was also Wilson's disciple. Liberal internationalism remained the core of America's foreign-policy establishment in academe as well as in government for the rest of the twentieth century. Students may follow part of its development by reading *On Active Service in Peace and War* (1948) by Henry L. Stimson, who was secretary of war between 1911 and 1913, secretary of state from 1929 to 1933, and again secretary of war from 1941 to 1945. The book was coauthored by McGeorge Bundy, who served Presidents John F. Kennedy and Lyndon B. Johnson as national security adviser from 1961 to 1966. Arthur Schlesinger Jr.'s 1995 article in *Foreign Affairs* titled "Back to the Womb?" may be this school's most recent self-definition.

Through the interwar period, under liberal internationalist Secretaries of State Stimson and Cordell Hull (1933–41), the nineteenth-century paradigm of foreign policy remained alive if suppressed within the Foreign Service, as one can see from the dispatches that Ambassador Joseph C. Grew sent from Tokyo trying to alert Franklin Roosevelt's administration to the disparity between the ends and means of its Japan policy. But the administration, supported amply by elite opinion, lumped the Foreign Service's views together with those of the America First Committee and the Anti-Intervention League, as expressions of selfish, immoral realpolitik. Since 1919, liberal internationalists had demonized the champions of that approach—Senator Henry Cabot Lodge and former president Theodore Roosevelt—for leading the American people to oppose the League of Nations. Now, as the establishment, they not only marginalized these views but even held them responsible for World War II. Students may wish to rent Darryl Zanuck's critically acclaimed movie *Wilson* (1944), in which Cedric Hardwicke plays the villainous Lodge.

Beginning in the 1940s, liberal internationalism's trunk began bending to the political left; many liberal internationalists judged that the American people had been insufficiently willing to align with the forces of progress in the world as represented by the Soviet Union and third-world movements such as Fidel Castro's Cuba. William Appleman Williams's text *The Tragedy of American Diplomacy* (1959) was seminal for the development of the subsequent generation of liberals, and shows how big that bend was. (Williams actually despised many of the original liberal internationalists.) Where the turn has led what is nowadays the larger part of liberal internationalism may be seen in *Legacy of Vietnam: The War, American Society, and the Future of U.S. Foreign Policy* (1976) by Anthony Lake, a member of President Nixon's National Security Council staff, national security adviser for President Bill Clinton, and an adviser to the 2008 presidential campaign of Barack Obama.

To some liberals, however, World War II meant that internationalism had ignored the *reality* of hostility among nations. These critics called themselves realists. Their principal text was Professor Hans Morgenthau's *Politics Among Nations*. First published in 1948, the book was assigned to more IR students than any other text for the rest of the century. In it, Morgenthau argues that all nations pursue their interest "defined in terms of power." By defining everyone's interests in a single term—*power*—realism, like the liberalism from which it springs, attributes the same motives to all peoples. But power to do what? Realist authors believe that governments and peoples are moved by incentives and disincentives ("carrots and sticks"). They assume that secure and, hence, limited gains are everyone's highest goal and that the balancing or moderation of one power by another and of one interest by another—that is, the balance of power—is something that nations seek for its own sake. They depict international relations as a process by which members of the international community maximize their interest by adjusting rationally to the realities of relative power.

In this way, rational choice theory and game theory sprouted from and intertwined with the realist branch. The realist academic canon also contains Robert Osgood's *Limited War: The Challenge to American Strategy* (1957), Thomas Schelling's *The Strategy of Conflict* (1960), and Henry Kissinger's *Nuclear Weapons and Foreign Policy* (1957). This canon promised maximization of interests for all sides by mixing competition with cooperation within matrices of rational choices. It empowered technocratic conflict managers over generals, and was a major part of the education of most of today's teachers of international relations

Especially during the last third of the twentieth century, realism led American statesmen to try harmonizing U.S. interests with those of its adversaries by trimming America's objectives in the expectation of reciprocity. But Kissinger confessed in *Diplomacy* (1994) that, by thinking this way, Americans ended up paying the same price for defeat in the Vietnam War that they would have had to pay for victory. In the same vein, Harold Brown,

President Jimmy Carter's secretary of defense (1977–81), summed up the result of restraining U.S. strategic weaponry through détente with the Soviet Union in the 1970s: "When we build, they build. When we stop, they build." President Gerald Ford stated in a 1976 debate with Jimmy Carter that U.S. policy acquiesced in the Soviet Union's domination of Poland (Ford thereby lost many Americans' esteem—and perhaps the presidential election). In the administration of George H. W. Bush (1989–93), Kissinger-disciple Brent Scowcroft and Secretary of State James Baker limited U.S. objectives in the Gulf War against Saddam Hussein's Iraq, in vain expecting that their restraint would lead Middle Eastern Muslim nations to recognize that their interest lay in a U.S. brokered general peace. Realists expected moderation to beget moderation. But these nations drew the opposite conclusion. In sum, realism acquired the reputation of failing to advance American interests and even failing to take due pride in America's peculiar nature.

Realism's practical results inspired neoconservatism. Beginning in the 1970s, Norman Podhoretz's *Commentary* magazine published distinguished liberals, including Georgetown professor Jeane Kirkpatrick and Harvard professor Daniel Patrick Moynihan, who rejected liberalism's assumption that all regimes are morally equivalent as well as realism's propensity to shortchange America's national interest. Not since Robert Taft's *Foreign Policy for Americans* (1951) had any prominent persons advocated the traditional American view that statesmen must act as the American people's fiduciary agents rather than as representatives of mankind. These authors also shared the vigorous anticommunism expounded in the editorial pages of the *Wall Street Journal* and by Ronald Reagan. This convergence of Wilsonian liberalism with conservatism came to be known as neoconservatism. "A neoconservative is a liberal who has been mugged by reality," said Irving Kristol.

The books that later made up the neoconservative canon showed clearly that its relationship to the statecraft of George Washington and John Quincy Adams was tangential. Joshua Muravchik's *Exporting Democracy: Fulfilling America's Destiny* (1991) and *The Imperative of American Leadership* (1996) argue that the primary purpose of America's national existence is to lead mankind into a new age of democracy. This task is feasible because the world's masses yearn for democracy, but delivering democracy necessarily requires all manner of interference in other nations' affairs to defeat mankind's oppressors. Robert Kagan's *Dangerous Nation* (2006) argues that this imperative predates Woodrow Wilson and is rooted in early American history. President George W. Bush's 2005 inaugural address encapsulated this sentiment: America cannot be free until all nations are free. No more succinct negation of America's original statecraft can be imagined. In short, neoconservatism should not be confused with *conserving* the America-centered foreign policy paradigm practiced between the administrations of George Washington (1789–97) and Grover

Cleveland (1893–97), or even with Theodore Roosevelt and Henry Cabot Lodge's alternatives to Wilsonian foreign policy (1913–21).

The student should note that liberal internationalists, neoconservatives, and realists in academe as well as in Washington share an intellectual premise problematic for understanding the world—namely, that all nations are actually or potentially of one mind with themselves. Thus liberal internationalists see foreigners as eager for modernization; neoconservatives see them as actual or potential democrats; and realists see them as pursuing enlightened self-interest, even when they are not. The point of studying international affairs, however, is to learn just how foreign peoples and polities actually *differ* from one another, as well as the ways in which they interact.

Making the most of your time in IR requires reading the best books, some of them quite old, which your professors may or may not assign—books that focus on the fundamentals: the characters in the great drama, the international stage on which they act, and the instruments they use.

THE STAGE AND THE CHARACTERS

❧

Understanding one's own country is the indispensable prerequisite for dealing with others. Necessarily, the way we deal with foreigners follows from how we understand what America itself is about, and generally how we believe we should relate to the rest of the world. How professors and books present international relations reflects their understanding of America implicitly. But because no IR curriculum teaches American history or institutions explicitly, serious students are well advised to read about and to understand America independently. Samuel P. Huntington's *Who Are We?* (2004) is a good place to start. The first two volumes of Walter McDougall's history of the United States—*Freedom Just Around the Corner* (2004) and *Throes of Democracy* (2008)—are indispensable.

THE STAGE

Ultimately, IR is about peoples and places that are very different. You must learn how deeply the global village's many neighborhoods differ from one another. Moreover, the maps that show the world divided into distinct states should not be taken to imply that the entities represented in the United Nations are nations in the dictionary meaning of the term, or that they are equivalent in any way. While no government can make "Bosnia" out of a place containing at least three warring tribes, the word "Japan" describes an entity that exists regardless of government.

Geography makes a difference. What are the soil and climate like? Is the topography steep or smooth, accessible by land or water? How numerous are the people? How young or old? What are their measurable characteristics? How many of them do what? What is in the people's heads, and what does that dispose them to do or not do? What do they worship, love, and hate? What is acceptable and unacceptable among them? How are they governed, what kinds of people among them set the tone for life, and what do they want? What is it like to make a living there and get ahead? What are their collective fears, hopes, and interests? What is their international agenda, if any? What "comparative advantages" do they have? What do they have to give and need to receive? What kind of power can they generate—how much, and for what purpose?

A good place to begin this tour of our planet is Sir Halford Mackinder's *Democratic Ideals and Reality* (1919), which shows geography's influence on politics. As you go through this classic introduction, refer often to a historical atlas as well as to specialized studies of individual regions.

Geography and Demography

Start from what Mackinder calls the "World Island"— namely, the Eurasian land mass plus Africa—beginning with its heartland, central Asia and Russia.

East of the Ural Mountains, Siberia's low ground, impassably wet and mosquito-infested in summer and frozen solid most of the rest of the year, slopes northward to the Arctic Ocean. Flowing from south to north, the Lena, Ob, and Yenisey rivers inhibit east-west traffic and are useful mainly as ice roads in the winter and for supply runs from the Arctic Ocean in the summer. Farming is inconceivable. Russia has long since overwhelmed northern Siberia's native nomadic tribes and has always used either slave labor or extraordinary incentives to exploit the region's vast timber and minerals. Oil and gas produced in self-contained camps flow out by pipeline. Siberia's southern edge is a gentle arc of higher ground that, in the west, touches the lower Volga valley and the Ukrainian plains, and that reaches eastward to the Amur River valley of the Pacific. This was the route by which Russia conquered central Asia and established itself on the North Pacific. Here, along the Trans-Siberian Railroad, are Russia's major eastern outposts: Novosibirsk, Irkutsk, and Vladivostok, as well as its intercontinental missile bases. This is also the route by which the Mongol peoples near its northeastern end conquered Russia, eastern Europe, and Asia in the thirteenth century.

Southward, east of the Caspian Sea, are the central Asian steppes and foothills of the great mountains, beyond which are China and the Indian subcontinent. Along the mountains' northern edge in today's Uzbekistan and Kazakhstan runs the Silk Road that once connected China with the Western world. Along this road came Tamerlane, the fourteenth-century Persian-Turkic successor to Genghis Khan, who conquered much of the area from Syria and Persia to the Volga River and India. The area's peoples—the Azeris, Kazakhs, Turkmen, Tajiks, Uzbeks, and Kyrgyz—retained their identity under Russian and Soviet rule, and have mixed Russian ways into their own. Because they are reproducing vigorously, unlike the Russians, they may well regain primacy in the region. Ted Rall's *Silk Road to Ruin* (2006) and Rene Grousset's *Empire of the Steppes* (1970) give tours of the area in our time.

Southwest of the Urals lie the vast lower valleys of the rivers Ural, Volga, Dnieper, and Don. In this fertile land, Russians mix with Ukrainians and Cossacks. Farther south, between the Caspian and Black seas, mountains divide the Caucasian Peninsula into climatically different valleys that separate peoples of different ethnicity, religion, and culture, among whom are the Christian Armenians, Muslim Azeris, Orthodox Georgians, Muslim Chechens, and countless other groups and subgroups. Since the sixteenth century, all of the above have been subjects of Russia's empire, from time to time, more or less. Vicken Chetarian's *War and Peace in the Caucasus* (2008) charts this historical labyrinth.

European Russia runs westward from the Urals as far as the Russian people have displaced others on the fertile northern European plain that reaches the Atlantic. On these western borders, Poles, Estonians, Latvians, Lithuanians, Ukrainians, Moldovans, and many others mingle with and dispute Russians, as do Finns in the north. Just as Russia's continental climate is known for polar cold and torrid heat, the Russian people are known for geniuses, peasants, and tyrants. But the land, the weather, and even the people's capacities cannot fully explain why Russia has dominated Eurasia under some regimes and merely become one of its parts under others, or why at one time it was one of the world's breadbaskets and has since become dependent on imported food. In our time, Russia's population is shrinking rapidly because fewer families are being formed and fewer children are born. Astolphe de Custine's *Journey for Our Time* (1839) is a good introduction to perennial Russia.

Russians have always looked hungrily at the Iranian plateau, and beyond the Caucasus and Anatolian highland to where the land falls steeply to the Persian Gulf and the warm Mediterranean Sea. In this junction of Asia, Europe, and Africa live the Persians, who mingled with and challenged Western civilization in its Greek and Jewish cradles, and the Turks, who have played a role in world affairs since they ended the Eastern Roman

Empire in 1453 and thereafter ruled nearly all Arabs and many eastern Europeans. Teetering between East and West, they remain strategically located atop the sources of the Middle East's scarce water supplies. The Iranians, too, have a history of dominating the Arabs, who live downhill from them, and an attitude to match. Rich in oil and gas, the Iranians live astride the routes by which the oil and gas of the landlocked Turkmen and Kazakhs must go to market. The substantial difference between the Iranians' and Turks' practice of Islam and that of most Arabs also shapes their complex relations with the Middle East. *The Middle East and North Africa: A Political Geography* (1985) by Gerald H. Blake and Alasdair Drysdale gives a good introduction to the region.

The Turkish-Iranian plateau feeds the streams that water the Middle East's Fertile Crescent—the irrigated areas that run northwest through desert from the Persian Gulf along the Tigris and Euphrates rivers through Mesopotamia (present-day Iraq) to northern Syria, and then south along smaller streams from Turkey and the Lebanese mountains into the Jordan Valley and Israel's coastal plain. The delta of the Mesopotamian rivers, the traditional home of the Marsh Arabs who practice Shia Islam, is rich in oil. In the Baghdad area between the rivers, the population includes some of the Sunni Arabs of Syrian or Bedouin heritage from the dry, western-northwestern flatlands. In the northern-northeastern mountains live the Kurds, whom Xenophon described in the fourth century B.C. and whose oil-rich territory includes parts of present-day Iran, Turkey, Syria, and Iraq. The clash of empires has been the history of this land, which once was agriculturally productive but whose growing population now eats mostly what it does not produce. Bernard Lewis's *The Shaping of the Modern Middle East* (1994) is essential.

In the Arabian Peninsula's vast desert between the Red Sea, Indian Ocean, and Persian Gulf, the European winners of World War I established the kingdom of Jordan to accommodate the Hashemite Arab princes—descendants of Muhammad and lords of the Hejaz (along the Red Sea where Mecca and Medina are located) who helped the Allies defeat the Turks but were themselves defeated by the Wahhabi tribes of the central Nejd valley under the Saud family. Since 1740, this family intermarried with and adopted the teachings of Abd-al-Wahhab, according to whom any perceived accretion to Islam's core monotheism disqualifies one as a Muslim and makes one lawful prey for true Muslims. Thus justified, the Saudi tribes have since controlled all but the northern part of the peninsula except for some British-protected emirates along the gulf coast and the primitive Yemeni tribes on the southern mountainous coast. Prior to the discovery of oil in the places dominated by Saudis, the Red Sea coast had been by far the peninsula's most economically viable area. For the Saudi kingdom's fast-growing population, however, prosperity relates directly to proximity to the royal family, whose custody of Islam's cradle—plus oil money—also lets it define Islam in Wahhabi terms for much of the Muslim world.

In Africa's northern bulge, the Sahara Desert forces humans to stay within a few moist margins on the Mediterranean, the Atlantic, and the Nile, or within the brush country on the edges of the central African forest. All around the great desert, population is growing faster than the production of food. Each of North Africa's human enclaves is different because each has been shaped by contact with different civilizations. Egypt is special. Orders of magnitude bigger than the others and heir to its own high civilization, Egypt worked its own compromises between Arabia's Islam and the Western world's modernity, thereby influencing northern Africa's whole eastern end. In Sudan in the upper Nile Valley, Muslim Arabs from the Egyptianized North oppress darker Muslims in the dry West, as well as black Christians and animists in the Blue Nile's wet, southern reaches. To the east, in the dry rugged highlands by the White Nile's headwaters, the Nilotic Ethiopians live with an ancient version of Christianity that had once flourished in flatland Egypt. Paul Henze's *Layers of Time: A History of Ethiopia* (2004) is a good place to start.

North Africa's Mediterranean coast, under Roman rule, provided grain and oil to Europe and produced Saint Augustine, arguably Christianity's foundational thinker. First the barbarian invasions, then Islam, returned the area to tribal ways and to poverty. When European powers displaced the Turks' nominal overlordship over present-day Morocco, Algeria, Libya, and Tunisia in the

1830s, they found the region little changed from centuries past. In the next hundred years, they reoriented North Africa toward Europe. Algeria especially became an integral part of France and a major exporter of wine. France, Germany, and Spain vied for influence in Morocco; France and Italy contended for Tunisia; and Italy sought control of Libya. But when these countries became independent, they stopped producing exports and started exporting refugees from misery. In our time, these lands teeter between secular despotism and Islamist despotism.

Maps of West Africa's muggy coast still carry names such as "Grain Coast," "Gold Coast," "Ivory Coast," and "Slave Coast, " which French and British colonists called the enclaves where they built modern cities including Abidjan, Accra, and Lagos. From these cities they spread civilizations that exported tropical products. Dakar, at the mouth of the Senegal River, was one of the world's major ports and had a Parisian cultural life. After the end of colonial rule, the area returned to tribal strife and poverty. Detritus from the decay and warfare of the interior tribes sinks into Africa's cities, where the diseases of modern slums compound the continent's endemic ones. Islam adds fuel to the wars between the interior tribes and the Christian coastal tribes. On the equator, the mighty Congo River cuts through otherwise impenetrable jungle all the way from the Atlantic to the Great Rift Valley, which divides the continent's East and West. But because the Congo falls too steeply and too near the ocean, like most of Africa's rivers, it does not let deep-draft ships into the wild interior valleys where tribal savagery trumps natural wealth. *Africa: The Land and the People* (1972) by Peter Duignan and Lewis Gann is a good introduction to the subject.

On the Great Rift Valley's eastern side are the cool lakes and fertile highlands of Uganda, Rwanda, Burundi, and Malawi. Further down gentle slopes toward the Indian Ocean are the temperate game-filled savannas and plantations of Kenya, Tanzania, and Zambia. In these hospitable environments, a mixture of Europeans and East Indians established peace and commerce between the mid-nineteenth and mid-twentieth centuries. But independence meant genocide between the Hutu and Tutsi tribes in the highlands, while in the foothills it meant the expulsion of the Indians, the marginalization of the whites, and the oppression of smaller tribes such as the Luo by bigger ones such as the Kikuyu. Similarly, the Shona and Ndebele tribes of the Zambezi Valley united to expel the whites from what had been prosperous southern Rhodesia, only for the Shona in turn to tyrannize and starve the Ndebele.

South of the Kalahari Desert, Africa's coastal plain enjoys a maritime climate at the crossroads of the Atlantic and Indian oceans. South Africa's Orange River valley is the continent's California. Above that, the Transvaal is endowed with rich minerals. Africa's southern tip was sparsely inhabited until the sixth century, when the major black Xhosa and Zulu tribes started moving into it from the North. "White tribes" of Portuguese, Dutch, and British rapidly expanded enclaves on the southern coast beginning in the seventeenth century. By the onset of black rule in 1994, four-fifths of South Africa's population was black, over one-tenth was white, and the remaining people were either East Indian or of mixed heritage. One-fifth of the white and East Indian populations emigrated right away, and more continue to do so. Prosperity has declined for all except those persons connected with the rulers. Nevertheless, South Africa's modern infrastructure keeps it, by far, the continent's largest producer of goods and services. Peter Duignan and Lewis Gann's *Hope for South Africa?* (1991) gives an optimistic but fact-based argument for how South Africa might avoid the rest of the continent's fate.

The ocean defines the sides of the strawberry-shaped Indian subcontinent. The Himalayas are the roof. Its west shoulder is the dry valley of the Indus River, which leads south from the mountains to the Arabian Sea near Karachi. The east shoulder is the soggy valley of the Brahmaputra River, leading south from the mountains to the monsoon-swept Bay of Bengal near Calcutta. In that vast delta also ends the Ganges River, which starts near the Indus and flows eastward under the mountains, along a valley that defines the subcontinent's North. A vast range of hills occupies the subcontinent's middle, intersected by countless smaller valleys. The bulk of the subcontinent's 1.3 billion people live in these valleys and along the coast, where the other major cities are located.

They speak some three hundred mutually unintelligible native languages and mainly share English. The Hindu among them are at least as mindful of their ethnic and caste identities as they are of Indian nationhood, while the Muslims and Sikhs define themselves by their religion. British rule from the eighteenth century to 1947 imposed uneasy peace among the majority Hindus and minority Muslims and Sikhs in a bewildering variety of local circumstances. As the British departed, they agreed to Muslim demands to create independent Muslim states in the Muslim-majority valleys of the Indus and Brahmaputra (West and East Pakistan, respectively). Millions of Hindus in these areas fled to Hindu India, while millions of Muslims in majority-Hindu areas fled westward to Indus-Valley Pakistan, or eastward to Bengali Pakistan, later renamed Bangladesh. Though millions of people are inured to dire poverty, millions of others have climbed out of it through exemplary work and study. O. H. K. Spate's *India and Pakistan: A General and Regional Geography* (1954) is a good place to start.

The highlands west of the Indus are the crossroads between the Indian subcontinent, central Asia, east Asia, and the Middle East. Here, in present-day Afghanistan, live the Pashtun, Baluch, Tajik, Uzbek, and Hazara, in tribes whose racial composition is the legacy of the empires that have come through central Asia to conquer India (Alexander the Great and the Mughals), or of those that have tried (the Russians). This real Afghanistan is not to be confused with the official one, whose borders divide each of these ethnic groups from their kin in neighboring states. Winston Churchill's first book, *The Story of the Malakand Field Force* (1898), is an enduringly accurate portrait of how people live in the highlands between the Indus Valley and Iran.

East and north of the Himalayas is Greater China, with more than a billion Han Chinese at its core, concentrated in the eastern end of the valleys of the Manchu, Yellow, Yangtze, and Xun Xi rivers. Most of the vast area culturally or militarily influenced by Chinese civilization—from Mongolia's mountains and steppes to Xinjiang's deserts, from Tibet's nosebleed heights to Indochina's lush forests and paddies—is inhabited by people related to the Han, racially and linguistically. Along the Amur River that separates Greater China from Russian Siberia, outside the Great Wall built to keep them out, live the Manchu, who conquered China in the seventeenth century and became part of it. Westward live the Mongols, who had the same experience in the thirteenth century. The western deserts below the passes to central Asia are home to the Muslim Uighurs; to their southeast, the Tibetans roam highlands as wide as coastal China. The river valleys that lead south from the mountains stretch to the tip of the Malay Peninsula, which guards the passage from the Indian Ocean to the Pacific. This is Indochina, inhabited by Thais, Khmers, Lao, Vietnamese, Malay, and countless subgroups. China's history has been one of centralized empire consistently undone by challenges from its parts. Those parts seem no less challenging in our time than they have ever been.

China's name for itself is *Zung Guo,* or "Center Country." Its dominant culture, a mixture of Confucian ethics and Buddhist spirituality, has influenced all it has touched. That culture includes the habit of obedience to authority, but it also includes appreciation of righteousness and intellectual curiosity. It has always been a fertile field for missionaries who preach freedom, and for despots who marshal slaves by the millions. Such is the fulcrum on which China's character and future balance. The fountainhead of the fabulous literature on China is the journal of Catholic missionary Matteo Ricci (1583–1610), best recounted in Vincent Cronin's *Wise Man from the West* (1955). Jonathan Fenby's *Chiang Kai-shek* (2004) is a good history of twentieth-century China.

Look next to the edges of the Eurasian landmass, to what Mackinder calls the "Rimlands": Japan, Oceania, the Americas, and Europe.

Japan is insular in more than just a geographic sense. A spine of earthquake-wracked mountains jutting out of the Pacific off Asia's coast, the Japanese islands provide scarce resources to the people who live there. Though its people are Sinotic in race, religion, and language, they see themselves as unique and the rest of the world as equally foreign. Disciplined, and fueled by a little rice and fish, the Japanese developed the skills first to fight off invaders, then to become the western Pacific's military hegemon in the first half of the twentieth century, and its economic powerhouse in the second. But in the twenty-first century, the well-fed, older Japanese people are declining in number and seemingly in international ambition. Robert C. Christopher's *The Japanese Mind* (1983) is a good place to start.

The Oceanic continent of Australia and New Zealand is also insular in more than the geographic sense. It consists of vast lands sparsely populated by prosperous white people but separated from the white world by the world's biggest ocean and by billions of tightly packed peoples of different colors and cultures, most of whom are poor. Dennis Rumley's *The Geopolitics of Australia's Regional Relations* (1999) lays out the hard facts.

The North and South American continents are almost literally a New World, where a mélange of immigrants from the Old World produced vastly different results in very diverse landscapes. A spine of tall mountains runs almost from the North to the South Pole along both continents' pleasant Pacific coasts. Deserts hug the mountains' western slopes near both tropics. In the temperate latitudes' Atlantic side, the land's elevation drops, rainfall increases, and agriculture thrives. While most of North America's most-hospitable zones lie in those latitudes, South America's are in its narrow southern cone.

Descendants of Europeans inhabit almost exclusively the Pacific and Atlantic sides of South America's temperate tip—Chile, Argentina, and Uruguay. Brazil's southern end, part of the temperate tip, has similar demographics and is the most prosperous part of that giant country.

Northward along Brazil's coast the population contains ever greater percentages of descendants of African slaves. In the country's Northeast, they are the predominant element, as on poor Caribbean islands. The Amazon River's hot, wet basin is a world unto itself, peopled by farmers, adventurers, government officials, and primitive tribes. The very high lands, whence flows the great river, were once home to the Inca Empire, which stretched from present-day Bolivia to Colombia. The Spanish conquistadores gave new masters to the empire's subjects, whose descendants are still the majority in this mineral-rich, but otherwise poor, region. On South America's steamy Caribbean coast live various mixes of indigenous people, blacks and whites. South America's abundance of natural resources has not meant prosperity.

The Spaniards who conquered North America's southern part did to the Aztec emperors what they had done to the Incas—they displaced them and took over their slaves. Since relatively few Spaniards emigrated to their Mexican empire, the population remained largely indigenous. By contrast, northward, in the lands that became the United States and Canada, just as in South America's southern cone, European immigrants came in such numbers and multiplied so quickly that they overwhelmed the natives. Temperate climate in what became the United States (nine-tenths of Canada's people live within one hundred miles of the U.S. border) helped the immigrants take advantage of abundant resources. But human factors, not physical ones, made the difference between the countries that European immigrants created in North America and those they left in the Old World, which often had even friendlier climates. The United States and Canada, nations made up of many nations, are the world's leading exporters of food. Their prosperity and coherence puts them in a class by themselves.

Geographically, Europe is merely the Eurasian continent's western cape. But its civilization and forms of governance distinguish it from the rest of the Old World as they distinguish it from the New World. Europe is divided geographically between its Balkan southeast, its Mediterranean south, its maritime north, and a northern plain that stretches from France to Russia. Just as important, it is divided between Eastern Orthodox and Latin Christianity, between traditions of absolute rule and of limited government, and between traditions of more or less state interference in economic life.

Since the seventeenth century we have been habituated to think of Europe's states as nations. It is by no means certain, however, to what extent the various peoples who compose each of these states retain the kind of common identity that statesmen of previous centuries forged when Welsh, English, and Scot became British; when Basque, Castilian, and Catalan became Spanish; when Bavarian and Mecklenburger became German; and when Lombard, Venetian, and Sicilian became Italian. In our time, ever more Europeans expect more and more from their central governments but are willing to give less and less to them because they recognize that their way of life is passing away. Europe's average birth rate of 1.4 children per woman, combined with the higher fertility and continued immigration of Muslims, guarantees that, fifty years hence, Europe's indigenous peoples will be an aging minority in what had been their lands. The student may profitably contrast Peter Duignan and Lewis Gann's *The Rebirth of the West* (1992), an account of western Europe's remarkable economic and social recovery in the generation after World War II, with books that describe Europe's subsequent development, such as Walter Laqueur's *The Last Days of Europe* (2009) and Bruce Thornton's *Decline and Fall: Europe's Slow-Motion Suicide* (2007).

CIVILIZATION AND THE CHARACTER OF NATIONS

Because a people's civilization is the most fundamental component of its character, there is no substitute for knowing and taking seriously the ideas and the history by which the major civilizations foster the mentalities and patterns of behavior peculiar to them. What does it mean for peoples to be part of a Christian (Latin or Orthodox), Confucian, or Islamic culture? Samuel P. Huntington's *The Clash of Civilizations and the Remaking of World Order* (1996) and Adda Bozeman's *Politics and Culture in International History: From the Ancient Near East to the Opening of the Modern Age* (1960) are good places to begin.

The world's civilizations flow from very different ways of viewing people's relationships with God, nature, and one another. We who have grown up in a Judeo-Christian civilization suppose wrongly that all mankind accepts that two contradictory propositions cannot be true at the same time in the same way and hence that grasping truth is possible and essential; that the human mind can grasp natural phenomena because they occur according to the laws of nature; that nature exists for man's use; that since men are neither animals nor gods, no man may treat another as if he were a god and the other an animal, and hence that all men are created equal; and that duties to God are different from duties to Caesar. *In fact, these propositions are indefensible, incomprehensible nonsense except in terms of the Hebrew Bible's Old and New Testaments and of Plato and Aristotle's teachings.* They are particular and exclusive to our civilization. The fact that persons raised in other civilizations now work calculus problems or make automobiles and nuclear weapons should not obscure the more important fact that their civilizations did not enable bright minds to conceive carburetors or imagine atoms. The fact that rulers in other civilizations sometimes respect their own laws does not mean they know that doing otherwise is wrong ipso facto.

Because each of the world's civilizations is an intellectual-moral universe that can be understood only in its own terms, cross-cultural communication is far harder than translating one language into another. Among the biggest mistakes that students and practitioners of international relations make is to assume that the words they hear in English from persons brought up in foreign cultures mean the same to them as they do to Americans—for example, that "freedom" is the same thing among people who believe that all men are created equal as among those who do not, or that "human rights" means the same thing to Jews and Christians, who believe that each human being is made in the image and likeness of God, as to those who do not. Moreover, civilizations, including our own, change as different ideas and emphases vie for prominence and as they adapt to contact with other civilizations. This means that the most consequential cultural clashes happen *within* civilizations rather than between them. Students and practitioners are well advised to discern to which *particular part* of his own civilization any given individual or group belongs. Changes in culture are most important because no way of life ever survives the death of the ideas that first gave it life.

Consider modern China. Its people dress in Western clothes and make their living manufacturing for the West with tools conceived in the West while listening to Western music. To the casual observer, historic China is no more. But very close to the surface is a layer of five-thousand-year-old habits of obedience to authority, devotion to family, and a hunger for order and learning, codified by two thousand years of Confucianism. No Chinese cultural authority distinguishes between what is right by nature and by convention. Just below that is another facet of Chinese civilization that runs partly counter to the first's tendency to limit the mind—

namely, individual curiosity about new ideas and things. By the turn of the twentieth century, the leaders of the Chinese people were steeping themselves in Western culture; the founder of modern China, Sun Yat-sen, and his successors developed syncretic versions of Christianity, republicanism, communism, and democracy. A glance at *Prescriptions for Saving China: Selected Writings of Sun Yat-sen* (1994), edited by Julie Lee Wei, Ramon H. Myers, and Donald G. Gillin, leaves no doubt about that. Today, China's nominal Communist Party rules over a remarkably free economy but, like China's historic imperial bureaucracy, tries to control the population tightly. Yet Chinese culture's inherent intellectual openness made it hospitable to missionaries who have kindled fires of Christianity that are spreading beyond anyone's control.

In our time, Islamic civilization is engaged in a civil war between political Islamism—Salafism, the Wahhabi sect, and the Muslim Brotherhood inhabit one corner, Islam's Hanafi and Sufi tendencies a second, and the Islamic world's Westernized elites a third. This struggle overlays the millennial conflict between Sunni and Shia, who are found in all three camps. Islam's core, besides strict monotheism, is the proposition that God dictated to Muhammad the Koran, which contains all that man needs to know or should know. This core limits the role of reason and the space for curiosity in Muslim lives, even though only the Sunni—not the Shia—deem it blasphemous to inquire about natural causes and effects.

Moreover, the Koran's specific commandments on political and social matters brand as heretical any laws not derived expressly from those commandments.

Islamic civilization's social-political aspects depend at least as much on the character of the peoples among whom Islam took root as they do on the Koran. Islam's original core of Bedouin tribes lived by *ghazw,* or *razzia*, killing other tribes' men, taking their goods, raping their women, and leaving them in the desert. Muhammad banned doing that to peoples who submitted to the One God. Thus Islam led peoples for whom humanity extended no farther than the tribe to agree that at least all Muslims are to be regarded as human beings. But for Muslims, the rest of mankind continues to live in *dar al harb,* the realm of war. Islamic civilization has always been divided by those who want to keep Islam close to its Bedouin roots and those who take the logic of monotheism further toward natural law, or those who are rooted in societies very different from those of the Arabian Desert. See, for example, Philip Carl Salzman's book *Culture and Conflict in the Middle East* (2008). Moreover, Islamic civilization has absorbed to some extent the gamut of Western civilization. Just as the Muslim world's liberals translate into Islamic terms the concepts of their Western brethren, so is the language of the Muslim Brotherhood replete with Marxist-Leninist concepts, and the audiotapes issued in the name of Osama bin Laden refer to "global warming." The logic of conflict seems to have trumped that of the Koran.

Hindu Buddhism does not distinguish between man and nature so much as it distinguishes between different castes of humans. That explanation of human society was sufficient for India's millennial civilization. But in our time, new concerns and divisions have arisen on that cultural assumption—enough to complicate, if not transcend, it. The English language infused Western civilization's British variant into the subcontinent's elite by becoming the vehicle for its education. While this education led some Indians (and Pakistanis) to imitate British bureaucracy and others to follow the West's cultural fashions, for millions of others it opened the possibility of personal achievement through academic excellence. Those who live in the new culture of individual achievement think in English and absorb at least some of the civilizational assumptions that the English language embodies. As that culture flows down society's ladder, the soil of Hindu civilization is producing hybrid plants.

Japanese civilization is not based on any religion. Shinto, its ancient religious practice, is animism without theology or philosophy. Buddhism left a residue of habits. Christmas decorations and the department stores' *Kurisumasu Seru* (Christmas sales) suggest that Christianity has made inroads into Japanese civilization, but it has not. Nor have inroads been made by the ideas that originated the Western technology by which the Japanese live in exemplary fashion. In fact, Japanese civilization has adapted other civilizations' features to its use so easily because none have touched its core: the belief that race and circumstance set the Japanese people apart from the rest of mankind. This civilization of a hundred million people worships itself, as small tribes do. Japanese culture changes—militaristic and prolific during the first half of the twentieth century, pacifist and shrinking in number during the second—but consensus and unity remain for it what custom is to Confucianism and the laws of nature and nature's God are to Judeo-Christian civilization.

Precisely because those laws are to be discovered and may be interpreted differently, Judeo-Christian civilization is inherently open and diverse. The fact that its basic premises—such as mankind's unique status in a created universe, human equality, and the imperative to discover truth and master nature—may be questioned from within those very premises puts it in a class by itself. In fact, the world's greatest struggles have taken place *within* Judeo-Christian civilization. Local factors also make Judeo-Christian civilization different, from Rome to Norway, from Poland to Chicago to Montevideo.

The ways of life most contrary to Judeo-Christian civilization have come from movements that sprang from it and made war from within. Medieval Gnostic sects and National Socialist and Marxist ideologies have led countless Europeans and Americans to assume the role of mankind's creators and, hence, to deny human equality. They have eschewed reason, seeking not to understand the world but rather to remake it. An exemplar of such movements in our time is the statement of a U.S. National Park Service ecologist: "Until such time as Homo Sapiens should decide to rejoin nature, some of us can only hope for the right virus to come along." This statement's equation of man with nature is not Buddhism. Nor does its desire to rid the world of millions of humans have anything to do with Hinduism, or with Kali, its goddess of death. Rather, modern environmentalism endows its adherents with the presumption that they are the planet's rightful gardeners who may do to weeds as they think best, and that most humans are alien weeds. How little different this logic is from that which has fed our civilization's totalitarian temptations since the Middle Ages may be seen by reading Norman Cohn's *The Pursuit of the Millennium* (1957).

Civilizations only set the boundaries. At any given time, in any given place, any people or individual will exhibit a peculiar mix of a civilization's traits. That is why it is incumbent upon students and practitioners of international relations to understand the complex individuality of each person and nation.

Regimes

The international personality of peoples—how they actually behave at any given time—depends much on how they are governed. Germany, for example, displayed different possibilities and played vastly different roles throughout the twentieth century, including the pre-1918 Wilhelmine monarchy, the Weimar Republic of the 1920s, the Nazi regime of 1933–45, and the 1950s'

Adenauer years; in our time, it is a sleepy member of the European Union. Japan and China, among others, have been sometimes passive and sometimes assertive, sometimes producers and other times destroyers of domestic wealth and international peace. Any country's role in international affairs depends on its internal character at any given time. That character, in turn, depends on who rules and for what purpose—in short, on the regime. My own book *The Character of Nations: How Politics Makes and Breaks Prosperity, Family, and Civility* (2009) is a good place to begin the study of current regimes.

Contemporary despotism exists in several varieties. The regimes of China and North Korea are what Karl Wittfogel describes in *Oriental Despotism* (1957): bureaucratically administered empires that Asia has known for millennia, which misapply the Western label "Communist Party" to their imperial retinues. Wittfogel argues that the Soviet Union itself was at least as much an oriental despotism as it was an enterprise out to change humanity. Whatever their purposes, and simply because they rule large areas and many people, modern despotic regimes—from Cuba and Venezuela to Algeria, Libya, Egypt, Syria, and Burma—are run by large parties that appoint, encompass, or override government officials. In smaller third-world countries, the rule is the despotism of one man's gang, as it was in antiquity.

Despotism at home does not necessarily mean aggression abroad. Even large Oriental empires often choose to look inward, as did the Chinese dynasties that built the

Great Wall, and as did the Japanese until 1868. Today, as ever, tyrannies typically prefer indirect strategies over wars that might bring a foreign power to bear on their inherently unstable domestic power. Hence, terrorism is the Middle East's weapon of choice. Even though the Soviet superpower waged proxy wars and held a military strategy that was all about seizing the offensive, its doctrine forbade offensive war because its Communist Party knew that its hold on the country was inherently shaky. In short, since despots are insecure, neither heroes nor madmen, they tend to make loud barks and take small bites, unless their prey shows provocative weakness.

Nearly all regimes nowadays call themselves "democracies" or "democratic republics." But since only Switzerland settles all serious issues by referendum, only that country is really a democracy. In the rest of Europe, the formalities of elections have seldom made much difference because parliamentary majority parties control government exclusively, because parties control elected officials, and because electoral politics have always been an overlay on the relationship between state bureaucracies and their clients. Though the United States has adopted Europe's bureaucratic model substantially, elections mean far more in America than in any other republic because the main political decisions are made by elected officials responsible only to their voters. Elsewhere, the self-designation "democratic republic" usually advertises that the country (e.g., the Congo) is a place where anything can happen *except* people ruling themselves.

Students and practitioners of international relations should note that the level of popular involvement in government is unrelated to a country's propensity to peace or war. In the ancient world, democratic Athens and Rome boldly conquered empires, while Sparta's military oligarchy stuck as close to home as it could. Democratic Switzerland is armed to the teeth, defensively. Europe's democratic nineteenth and twentieth centuries were bloodier than its previous monarchical centuries because its peoples proved more bloody-minded than its kings had been. Contemporary European pacifism is evidence not of any inherent democratic penchant for peace but rather of the fact that democracy reflects the character of any *demos* and of its regime, and that today's European peoples and regimes are pacifist. Alexander Hamilton summed up the matter in *Federalist* 6: "There have been . . . almost as many popular wars as royal wars. The cries of the nation and the importunities of their representatives have, upon various occasions, dragged their monarchs into war."

Many of the world's regimes are of, by, and for small, self-selected groups. Iran's "Islamic Republic" is the only one of these that might lay a slender claim to the title "aristocracy," because it vests supreme authority in a Council of Guardians chosen by wise clerics who are supposed to choose people wiser than themselves. But since these rulers rule more for personal wealth than for virtue, and since they rely increasingly on mercenary security forces their regime is best thought of as an oligarchy, like so many others. Among these are the oligarchies of Saudi Arabia and the United Arab Emirates, whose nominal monarchs function as chairmen of the board of family enterprises run for the families' pleasure.

The distinction between despotism and oligarchy matters to students and practitioners of international relations because it points to the practical questions of who really governs, how the regime may be influenced, and where the levers are by which it can be moved. Whereas the regimes we call despotic are controlled coherently from a single source from which all their members derive their power, oligarchies are coalitions of people who are powerful in their own right. Whereas despotisms have single agendas, oligarchies have as many as they have factions. The more self-sufficient the factions, the closer the oligarchy is to feudalism. Machiavelli describes the Turkish Empire as "governed by one lord, the others are his servants," and contrasts this regime with countries like feudal France, where "always one finds malcontents." While anyone "can enter [into France] with ease," anyone attacking a Turkish-style despotism must depend more "on his own forces than on the disorders of others" (*The Prince*, chapter 4). Machiavelli's operational judgment on oligarchy and feudalism applies even more strongly to what are usually called democracies.

How particular selections from a civilization's cultural menu and the particular choices of leaders produce particular regimes is far beyond our scope. Students and practitioners of IR must note each regime's individual character, objectives, strengths, and weaknesses, and keep in mind Hamilton's warning in *Federalist* 6: "The causes of hostility among nations are innumerable . . . the love of power or the desire of preeminence . . . jealousy . . . equality and safety . . . the attachments, enmities, interests, hopes and fears of leading individuals . . . personal advantage or personal gratification."

THE INTERNATIONAL SYSTEM
IN HISTORY

ॐ

The international system—that is, the system in which nation-states recognize the sovereignty of other nation-states, distinguish sharply between peace and war, and deal with one another through ambassadors whose immunity they guarantee—dates only to the 1648 treaties of Westphalia, which ended the wars of the Reformation by pledging mutual noninterference in internal affairs. In our time, the system does not exhaust what actually happens among peoples and is evolving constantly away from the classic model. Increasingly, regimes blend war and peace and challenge the sovereignty of other nations through nonstate actors and international institutions.

Although this survey follows Western history for the most part, it is essential for students to be aware of the Persian, Indian, and Chinese classics of statecraft. Each reflects its own civilization and predominant regimes. Persia's *Shahnameh,* the Book of Kings, is a guide to the conspiracies of imperial courts. India's *Arthasastra* describes the art by which some men gain power over others. Sun Tzu's *Art of War* is a set of insights into human conflict. Interestingly, while these classics are commensurate with Western ones in their treatment of the dynamics of power, none deals with the role of power in the establishment of peace. By contrast, peace and order have always been central to the Western understanding of statecraft.

Surely the most instructive of books in international relations, Thucydides' *History of the Peloponnesian War*, tells of the struggle between Sparta and Athens, the great powers of fifth-century Greece, waged in the shadow of the Persian Empire. The Greek cities' many peace treaties succumbed to mutual fears, clashing interests, and hunger for honor.

Thucydides shows that because none of the belligerents aimed at a peace with which all could live, this great war had only losers. The Hellenic world had civilized itself during centuries of peace and order, but the Greeks dissipated in war the strength and decency built up in peace. Each side made war in ways that reflected what had first made them great. Thucydides shows how Athens's poor soil had fostered its democracy and seafaring, while Sparta's domestic concern with its Helot underclass determined its behavior. Especially when read in the light of the contrasts Herodotus draws between oriental empire and Greek polity, Thucydides' account fixes the reader's mind on the primordial fact that the international personality of any people reflects its domestic identity.

Thucydides' account of the politics, diplomacy, strategy, and operations of the war may well be the most thoughtful lessons ever written on the instruments of statecraft. It has taught countless generations of statesmen. By itself, it is a complete education in international affairs. Any time that students might take from other books to ponder this one would be well spent.

The idea that peoples could live side by side in peace, their intercourse governed by law, arose not out of any balance between independent cities but rather out of the Roman Empire. *Jus Gentium*, the Law of Nations, set rules by which the empire's various parts could resolve disputes and press claims. Later, along with Christian canon law, *Jus Gentium* became the effective international system of the Western Middle Ages. Its essence was that Christendom's various princes, cities, and myriad entities recognized that each had legitimacy, that the principal job of each was to be a *defensor pacis* (defender of the peace), and that they were obligated to negotiate claims against one another or to submit them to superior authorities. These medieval negotiators' credentials were called *diplomae.* The *diplomati* who bore them were effectively lawyers who argued a client's case on the basis of common texts and customs. This is not to say that relations between medieval princes were very peaceful, but only that there existed the intellectual basis, the *presumption,* that peace and law-based order should govern relations between princes.

A century before the Protestant Reformation of 1517, and two centuries before the 1648 treaties of Westphalia gave birth to the modern international system, that presumption was undermined by conflicts between the Holy Roman Emperor and the papacy, within the papacy itself (at one point in the fourteenth century there were three popes), and between the emperor and his electors; it was also undermined by the rise of kings in England, Spain, and France. By 1576, when Jean Bodin's *Six Books of the Republic* explained "sovereignty," these kings already recognized no authority higher than their own. Garrett Mattingly's *Renaissance Diplomacy* (1955) is the best place to begin understanding the transition from diplomats who worked, at least theoretically, as representatives of a body of law common to all, to diplomats who served as representatives of amoral sovereigns. The most profound explanation of the modern state's relationship to right and wrong is found in Machiavelli's *The Prince* and *Discourses,* and in Thomas Hobbes's *Leviathan.*

The international system is not a community of nations. Few of its member states actually represent nations; rather, they represent peoples who would prefer to be apart. Moreover, the system provides very narrow common ground.

The kings of Spain, France, and Sweden; the Dutch Republics; the Swiss Confederation; and the German princes promised at Westphalia in 1648 not to interfere with one another's internal affairs, primarily to remove external obstacles to the sovereignty that each was trying to establish over heterogeneous territories. Thenceforth the world's European epicenter would be assumed to consist of sovereign, homogeneous nation-states that recognized one another as such. The Westphalian system of mutual recognition became universal in the ensuing three centuries, as all European sovereigns joined it and then appended to it the colonies they established in Asia, the Americas, and Africa. Eventually, they recognized as sovereign nation-states the independent regimes of their ex-colonies, as well as the regimes in parts of the world that Europe never conquered such as China, Japan, and Ethiopia. Thus by the mid-twentieth century the world's map was neatly divided into differently colored pieces, assumed to be nations. In fact, few of these states—including Europe's—are homogeneous nations. Ethnic conflicts challenge most sovereignties from within.

The international system's common ground is narrow because it is based on the substitution made by the treaties of Westphalia of individual states' *sovereignty* for the common standards of Christian canon and customary law that had ruled relations among Europeans since the days of Charlemagne. While the great commentaries on the new system, Hugo Grotius's *De Jure Belli ac Pacis* (*On the Laws of War and Peace,* 1625) and Emmerich de Vattel's *Law of Nations or the Principles of Natural Law* (1758), drew as much as they could from the Roman *Jus Gentium,* nevertheless the signatories of Westphalia had only agreed not to interfere in the internal affairs of other nations, and to abide by their promises. Modern *international law* is neither more nor less than the sum of those promises—treaties, conventions, agreements, and customs.

Because sovereignty is the system's primordial feature, each nation is *equal only in its sovereign right* to judge what it owes and is owed. In theory as well as in practice, modern promisers keep promises as long as they find it convenient to do so, and to the extent that the promisees make it inconvenient not to do so. Insofar as an international system exists, it does so by virtue of each government's recognition of the absolute freedom of choice of other governments. That freedom can be abridged by treaties and conventions, *but the mutual recognition of sovereignty that gives the international system a measure of existence is also precisely what limits that existence.* So the web of agreements known as international law binds any given government only insofar as it wants to be bound, or as another government forces it to be.

That is why, as John Quincy Adams taught, sovereigns' interests may be *parallel* but are never common. Nor does any amount of intercourse commonality make. Because *sovereign autonomy is the essence of international law,* it cannot prevent states from harming, or even annihilating, one another. Thus in 1795, even when the "international community" consisted of a few European Christian kings, this community calmly eliminated Poland from the map. In 1914, when most of Europe's sovereigns were related to one another, they fought the Great War, which set the tone for our bloody time.

International institutions are creatures of agreements among governments that governments and interest groups often use to bypass their own and others' domestic institutions. Some, such as the International Air Transport Agency, exist by necessity. Others, such as UNESCO (United Nations Educational, Scientific, and Cultural Organization), exist as balancing acts between the agendas of states. Others yet, such as the Intergovernmental Panel on Climate Change (IPCC), advance agendas which parties and interest groups find difficult to pursue in their several countries. The United Nations' human-rights panels have been instruments of ideological war against Judeo-Christian civilization. For instance, the 2001 World Conference against Racism (WCAR), held in Durban, South Africa, and led by Muslim countries and other despotisms, indicted Israel and the United States. In 2008 one of the UN's panels released a report approving of "acts committed in the course of a war of national liberation against apartheid, colonialism or military occupation"; Israel's "Judaization" of Jerusalem was given as the prime example of a provocation to be legitimately resisted with violent acts.

To understand the United Nations, students must distinguish between its agencies—some of which would exist regardless of whether or not they were under any umbrella organization—and the structure of the General Assembly and Security Council. It is essential for students to be acquainted with the grandiose hopes invested in the founding of that structure and those agencies, and with how diametrically their reality diverges from those hopes. The student may well begin with the contrasting accounts of two U.S. diplomats: Robert Murphy's *Dip-*

lomat Among Warriors (1964) and Dean Acheson's *Present at the Creation* (1969). *ConUNdrum: The Limits of the United Nations and the Search for Alternatives* (2009), edited by Brett D. Schaefer, considers the marginal role that the UN plays in day-to-day international affairs.

Day-to-Day International Affairs in Our Time

We can grasp the complexity of modern international affairs by dividing them along the categories of international law: private, administrative, and constitutional or political. Most transactions across borders are by, of, and for private individuals or companies. Whereas anyone doing business in a foreign county must do so on that country's terms, those terms are often governed by international treaties and almost always subject to customary reciprocity. Indeed, reciprocity is the great, ultimate enforcement mechanism of private international law. It is the reason why, most of the time, *private* international law "works." Necessity makes *administrative* international law work: Nobody forces pilots who fly international routes to speak a common language. They all speak English, or try, because all know that trying to land at an airfield without communicating with the tower would be deadly. For the same reason, governments that place satellites in the limited spaces available in geosynchronous orbits would rather check their plans with the International Telecommunication Union than risk collisions.

The very idea of *political* international law is problematic in our time, given that today's 190-odd states have less in common, arguably, than did the tribes that contended for power during the Dark Ages. The difference between the international political system at the beginning of the twentieth century and the same system at the beginning of the twenty-first century is stark. Paul Johnson's *Modern Times* (1983) shows how the international system came to be as it is.

As late as 1912, former U.S. secretary of state Elihu Root received the Nobel Prize for proposing a system of arbitration that would subject international disputes to the rule of law, enforced by the consensus of the dominant Protestant Christian nations of the time. After these had fought a disastrous, pointless war, American and British statesmen at the 1919 Versailles Peace Conference imagined that a "League of Nations" would enforce rules common to a wider group of "civilized nations," assuming that common civilization would trump divisive issues. Thus they brokered the birth of unnatural, unsustainable entities, from Danzig to the Danube, from Prague to Palestine, from Adriatic Istria to Arab Iraq. Alas, these unprecedented *pledges of common purpose* involved *more* nations with *less in common* than before. Nevertheless, Euro-American statesmen ever since have invested more hopes in an imaginary international community based on shared aspirations.

The United Nations is supposed, by many, to embody mankind's shared aspirations and its governments' compatible objectives. But our statesmen falsified their own supposition by wanting the Soviet Union to be one of the UN's pillars even though most knew that its aspirations and objectives were contrary to any civilization. They also formally opened the UN to any state, provided the state be "peace loving," though that requirement was, and remains, a fiction. The Communist states charged that the very existence of non-Communist governments was a threat to peace. Pretense aside, the UN's founders really intended that the only qualification for membership in the international community be de facto government *power, stripped of any ethical or political content.* But they ended up abandoning that qualification as quickly as they had previous ones.

By 1993, the logic of defining its community to include those most troublesome to it led the UN General Assembly to confer upon Yasser Arafat—leader of a band that bombed school buses and murdered U.S. ambassadors, Olympic athletes, and airport passengers—the status supposedly reserved to heads of peace-loving states. The UN recognized Arafat's sovereignty over the "Palestinian Authority," hoping this might *moderate* him. *Moderation*—or at least the hope of moderation—had become the final pretend-criterion for membership. But the standard for measuring moderation turned out to be hope driven by fear. That combination lowered the standard for membership. Hence, in today's UN, Saudis lecture Americans about religious toleration, Iran sits on the Commission on the Status of Women (CSW), and such despotisms as Libya and Sudan help define the meaning of "human rights" for the "international community."

In a nutshell, political international relations in our time are contests not only over relative power and primacy but also over what behavior is acceptable and what is unacceptable—ultimately over which regimes and ways of life are legitimate or not. Modern international politics no longer accepts the Westphalian assumption that no government may interfere in another's internal affairs. Whereas a hundred years ago, and even up to our own time, many of our statesmen and academics imagined that they and the traditional European members of the international community could set international standards, the Soviet Union pioneered the contention that Euro-Americans must pay a price—material, moral, and behavioral—to be considered "peace-loving" states or "progressive" states. A host of successors have continued to goad the international community's original members to grant demands for transfer of resources to non-Euro Americans in the name of good international citizenship. Indeed, even among Euro-Americans, the notion that "our interest" in international affairs includes dictating the internal affairs of other peoples is not uncommon. It is no surprise, then, that contemporary international politics consists so heavily of the application of the instruments of power.

THE INSTRUMENTS OF POWER

❧

To understand the instruments of power—diplomacy, economic favors and sanctions, acts of subversion, and military force—practitioners and students alike must view these instruments in the context of policy objectives and strategies for achieving those objectives. Few errors are as common or as grave as is the error of treating these instruments *as strategies or policies, never mind as ends in themselves.* It follows that any of these instruments, however well employed on its own terms, is useful only insofar as it is combined with the others in the service of strategy, policy, and objectives.

Though countless books have mystified the term "strategy" or confused it with any given action, strategy is best understood as any reasonable set of plans for using the means at hand to achieve the ends of policy. Strategy is a plan for getting from here to there; it is the concrete art of balancing ends and means. Policy is also concrete: it is the opposite of wish lists and antipathies. Rather, as Charles de Gaulle reminds us, policy is an "ensemble of continued pursuits, of decisions matured, of measures brought to term." Both policy and the strategy for its implementation are to be measured against the statesman's objectives. Judging these is surely the statesman's most crucial task. While reasonable objectives may be pursued through better or worse policies and strategies, ill-chosen objectives *guarantee* counterproductive policies and unreasonable strategies.

In sum, the arts of diplomacy, economic suasion, influence, and war are *means by which to move other countries.* They are logically subordinate to decisions about the *ends* proper to one's own country and prudent in its circumstances.

Diplomacy

Diplomats' words will persuade competent foreign officials insofar as they represent a compelling reality. From this, two often-neglected axioms follow. First, diplomacy is neither more nor less than the *content* of the messages it conveys. No error could be greater than to think that the diplomatic *process* has any value independent of its substance. Second, because reality drives events, *diplomacy is about truth,* precisely conveyed. Attempting to misrepresent reality casts doubts on your strengths and highlights your weaknesses.

Most of the intercourse among the world's diplomats imitates the transaction of business: two sides meet knowing what each wants from the other, and knowing that the other is more or less willing, and able, to give what is asked for, more or less for the price proffered. As in business, the negotiator's skill lies not in any artifice but rather in ensuring that both sides have an accurate picture of what the other brings to the table. But in some of the most important diplomatic relationships, in which the objectives of the two sides are *not* mutually compatible, different rules apply. An essential part of the diplomat's art consists of judging whether *this* negotiation can reasonably aim at accommodation, or whether the objectives of the two sides are so mutually exclusive that diplomatic contact naturally serves belligerent "side effects"— the opportunity to gather intelligence, deceive, gain time, mobilize support from third parties, or weaken the other government's domestic front. Fred C. Iklé explains this best in *How Nations Negotiate* (1968).

In formulating negotiating positions, the wise diplomat crafts offers that, if accepted, would require the other side to give up relatively little in exchange for a greater benefit, but, if refused, would make it liable to disproportionately greater harm. Such offers cannot reasonably be refused—so long as they represent reality.

Public Diplomacy and Prestige, or "Soft Power"

Peoples (and governments to a lesser extent) are moved by affections and enmities, by fears and honor, as well as by interests. This has led many to imagine that the management of popular passions, what some now call "soft power," can substitute for the ordinary tools of statecraft. But the concept of soft power, which stresses what is attractive to contemporary Western elites, oversimplifies the role of ideas and contradicts historical experience. Students and statesmen must grasp the real power and limits of ideas.

Machiavelli's tongue-in-cheek disparagement of "unarmed prophets" notwithstanding, some of history's most important events—Christianity's conquest of the Roman Empire, Christian-classical civilization's subsequent conquest of the barbarian tribes which had overrun Europe, and Chinese civilization's victory over Kublai Khan's Mongol conquerors—happened over centuries as more attractive ways of life triumphed over superior military power. Every great empire has combined military power and policy prudence with attractive ideas of how people should live. By contrast, today's notion of soft power, most fully elaborated by Joseph Nye's *Soft Power* (1990), supposes that a nation's innocuousness and propensity to please are attractive enough to reduce or eliminate the need for statecraft.

Yet ideas, important as they are in the long run, do not cancel the effects of military or any other kind of force in any concrete instance. As Hans Morgenthau pointed out, prestige is having a reputation for power, for successfully weighing on events, for having to be taken seriously, for possessing what the Romans used to call *gravitas*. By the same token, incapacity or unwillingness to protect friends and to put enemies out of action engenders contempt. Moreover, peoples are moved even more powerfully by hate and fear than they are by attraction. By far the most potent ideas in international affairs are the ones that relate to any people's identity. Even religion, the essence of which is man's relationship with the supernatural, often moves nations because they identify their own gritty circumstances with a particular form of worship.

Successful statesmen have always known the importance of appealing to minds and hearts. Governments at war try to separate their opponents from their peoples by appealing to those peoples. During the Cold War, such "public diplomacy" was of substantial importance because the Soviet empire's populations were prisoners of their own governments and would rather have been living under Western governments. But regardless of the situation, any government helps its own cause by explaining to others (*and, not incidentally, to itself and to its own population*) what it is doing and why.

Successful appeals to minds and hearts must reflect the audience's interests, not yours or your own country's. Before the audience listens to you about anything else, it wants to know what your country is doing to preserve what *it* values and to undo *its* enemies, because your country's determination to advance its own values and interests is a guarantee of the integrity of its international commitments. That is why it is imperative that foreign commitments flow naturally from what each country's own people really want. Such appeals have to be verified by actions and ratified by success. The essays in *The Battle for Hearts and Minds: Using Soft Power to Undermine Terrorist Networks* (2003), edited by Alexander T. J. Lennon, explain why U.S. foreign policy has counted on appeals to hearts and minds, relegating military actions to a supporting role, from the Vietnam War of the 1960s to Afghanistan in 2010. While hearts and minds are moved by success, however, *they do not produce it.* Failure repels viscerally.

ECONOMIC STATECRAFT

Economic favors and strictures are blunt tools. While bribery may be effective on occasion, the rule is that it is easier to buy foreign leaders than to make them stay bought. Seldom will money move foreigners to risk their domestic political base, never mind their lives. While economic sanctions can be powerful adjuncts to war, and even the threat thereof may cause compliance if the cost of complying is lower than that which the sanctions would impose, sanctions cannot force compliance with demands if compliance would damage the regime or its important objectives. Regimes—especially authoritarian ones—can simply shift the burden of sanctions onto the sectors of their population that are least important to their objectives.

Economic warfare can be deadlier than atom bombs. The Allied blockade in the First World War killed more

Germans than did the Allied armies on all fronts. But because goods are fungible, measures of economic warfare must be applied wholesale. Because trade with third countries can circumvent sanctions, effective economic warfare must also target any nation that trades with the target nation. To be serious, any act of economic warfare toward any nation must risk conflict with the rest of the world. *In short, serious economic sanctions are not cheap, while cheap ones are not serious.*

Economic incentives can be decisive when they add to the effects of well-conceived military and political pressures in ways that cement the correct impression that further resistance is futile as well as painful. But when economic incentives are applied in lieu of decisive measures, simply to prod or to punish, they become counterproductive because they convince the target government that its adversary is capable of nothing more. Japan interpreted the U.S. economic sanctions of 1940–41 in this way, concluding that America would take Pearl Harbor lying down.

Using economic incentives to "send a message" of moderate pressure risks having the message misinterpreted. Pericles of Athens may have imposed economic sanctions on neighboring Megara to punish it for shifting its alliance to Sparta as a moderate way of warning other allies not to follow suit. His intention was not to provoke Sparta to defend its new ally. But Sparta used these sanctions as the excuse for declaring war on Athens. David Baldwin's *Economic Statecraft* (1985) is the best one-volume study of this often-used, but little-understood, tool of statecraft.

SUBVERSION

Notwithstanding international law's presumption that all states are sovereign, governments have never ceased to interfere in one another's internal affairs as part of normal relations, not just of hostilities. After all, influencing foreign governments is the proximate reason for dealing with them. What some regard as friendly influence others will denounce as hostile, subversive interference.

To understand subversion as a tool of statecraft, the student must begin by putting aside the popular notion that it is essentially a secret activity carried out by special agents. Instead, focus on three facts: First, any and all societies include people who are likely to be unsympathetic to their government's policies or to their government itself. All governments and societies are made up of persons whose individual opinions and interests may make them independent actors to some extent. Wise statesmen always take such internal divisions into account and cultivate allies in foreign camps. Second, diplomacy, economics, and military activities are natural instruments for leveraging such contacts. Third, while some of the modalities of this leveraging may be secret, subversion is a kind of seduction—no one has ever been seduced or subverted without some degree of cooperation. The success of subversion depends less on the subverter's skill than on the target's susceptibility—on how it manages its internal differences. Subversion is most effective when the dissidents believe themselves to be, and are, independent advocates of policies that are appealing in and of themselves rather than mere tools of a foreign power.

Subversion is endemic. One country may subvert another politically just because its existence offers the other's dissidents inspiration. For instance, the United States has inspired countless people across the globe to regard the political order in which they live as inferior by comparison, and to aspire for something better. Similarly, the Soviet Union's existence inspired many influential Americans to see it as the harbinger of justice in the world, and to regard socialism a way of life to be emulated in America. More or less openly, with material and diplomatic means, the United States, the Soviet Union, and many other governments have supported like-minded individuals and groups in foreign countries. Such support makes possible a degree of control by one country over another, and makes it proper to speak of such subversives as agents of a foreign power. But experience has shown that the more a country emphasizes control of its foreign allies, and the more it tries to substitute its agenda for theirs, the less effective these allies become.

Economic subversion—that is, either positive or negative inducements to specific individuals or groups within the target country—can be highly successful. France's King Louis XIV controlled English foreign policy by making "pensioners" of many of England's court, including King James II. Nor have Saudi monarchs wasted their money as they spread largess in Washington and Houston among persons influential with administrations of both parties. By contrast, Henry Kissinger's attempt in the 1970s to bind the Soviet Union through a network of politically constraining commercial deals failed because Soviet officials were not amenable to subordinating collective political ends to individual material gains—especially since they learned they could have both.

Force, and even the prospect thereof, can be most subversive. If a government can be convinced that resistance to demands will only result in a war it will surely lose, it is likely to give in. In 1954, when the United States convinced Guatemala's socialist president, Jacobo Arbenz, that it would do whatever was necessary to ensure the success of a rebel army, he fled the country. But no potent rebel army existed. The United States used subversion precisely because it was *not* willing to do whatever was necessary. Had Arbenz not panicked, had he measured the forces actually arrayed against him, he would have retained the mastery of the situation that he actually possessed. In 1961, when a U.S.-backed rebel force landed at Cuba's Bay of Pigs, Fidel Castro correctly judged that he could defeat it and that the United States was not serious. The lesson here is that any use of force is truly subversive when it is decisive in and of itself, or when it really augurs the use of even greater and more decisive force.

Arming and inspiring a foreign country's dissidents to wage guerrilla warfare or commit acts of terrorism may weaken it, dispirit it, and cause it to change policies or even governments. In 2004, Sunni Arabs who were fighting the U.S.-led occupation of Iraq worked with the terrorists in Spain who bombed Madrid's commuter trains to bring about the electoral defeat of the government that had joined the U.S. coalition and replace it with a government that removed Spanish troops from Iraq.

The subversive effect of violence, just like the subversive effects of enhanced political dissidence and economic incentives, depends less on the means employed than on the target country's susceptibility. Guerrillas or terrorists are tools of indirect war. They succeed insofar as the target country chooses not to identify their sponsors as belligerents and to wage war against them. After all, chances are that the countries that sponsor them do so because they are unwilling to wage war directly.

WAR

Choosing and managing war and peace is the ultimate test of statesmanship. War is not only a tool that peoples use to adjust their place among others; it is also the means by which most nations are born and die. Every war, no matter how small it may appear at the beginning, is a matter of life and death. Its violence looses passions, calls into question all of the participant nations' reasons for being, and provides additional incentive and leverage to each regime's domestic enemies. War places all the contenders' existence in the balance. Few subjects are as understudied in our colleges as is war—and few subjects are as important. Nevertheless, many books give adequate introductions to the field. Among these are Donald Kagan's *On the Origins of War and the Preservation of Peace* (1995) and *War: Ends and Means* by Angelo Codevilla and Paul Seabury (second edition, 2006).

There are as many kinds of wars as there are peoples, regimes, and objectives. Tribal warfare aims at annihilating enemy peoples or enslaving them, or at least at driving them from the land that the tribe wants to occupy. In the ancient world, the losers' gods were shattered, their men put to the sword, and their women and children sold as slaves. The German-Soviet front in the Second World War was this kind of war. From the sixteenth through the eighteenth centuries, African tribes made war on each other to see who would sell whom to Arab slave wholesalers. By contrast, wars in civilized eighteenth-century Europe were for limited stakes and involved few noncombatants. But World War I and the Peloponnesian War are examples of conflicts among civilized opponents whose initial objectives were trampled by the logic of the war itself: ultimately, these conflicts involved whole civilizations and changed the character of all involved. The particular combatants' character and objectives—not technology—determine each war's destructiveness.

War consists of the bloody commitment to destroy an enemy or force him to accept one's own version of peace. The timing, focus, and degree of violence to be used depend on strategy. The Soviet Union, for example, never declared war on its "enemies" in the West, and it certainly never attacked them, even though it understood itself to be at war with them from its inception to its demise. Rather, the Soviet Union pursued their destruction largely through subversion and indirect warfare, building the most intimidating armed forces possible and elaborating frighteningly reasonable plans for military victory. By contrast, the British and French declaration of war against Germany in September 1939, provoked by Germany's conquest of Poland, was a phony war because the British and French had no intention of doing what was necessary to free Poland. There was, however, nothing phony about the Germans' attack on France and Britain in 1940.

Not all international violence amounts to war. Occupations are not war. Neither do efforts at nation building amount to war.

Military operations, regardless of size or casualties, amount to war only if they serve reasonable plans for achieving a country's preferred state of peace. In this sense, although Napoleon was a master of battles, he failed at war because his masterly moves were not well aimed at a state of rest. Though it is impossible to foretell the consequences of any war, statesmen worthy of their offices go to war only after being clear about the peace at which they aim; who or what stands in the way of that peace; the military and other operations that, if successful, will remove that obstacle; and their own capacity and commitment to carry out those operations. Without such calculations, war's violence is truly senseless.

While authors from Thucydides to Carl von Clausewitz in *On War* (1832) have described both war's irrational and rational sides, an influential modern school of thought regards war as *entirely* irrational in our time. Norman Angell's *The Great Illusion* (1910) argued that no major power would start a war because modern weapons had made war so destructive that it would produce no gains for anyone. Four years later, events proved that modern war was even more destructive than Angell had imagined, but that peoples were all too eager to fight for no gain at all. Martin Van Creveld's *The Transformation of War* (1991) won converts in Washington, as well as on campuses, with the message that only people moved by such irrationalities as ethnicity or religion would make war in our time. Since these people would make war without a clear calculus of ends and means, Western statesmen should recast their own armed forces as constabularies to suppress the irrationals. This school of thought assumes that all states have a common interest in suppressing "violent extremism."

But states and regimes do have clashing interests; violence—whether in the form of armies crossing borders or of terrorists making life unsafe within them—is a tool eminently useful to reason. The so-called irrational or rogue persons who carry out acts of intimidation do so to move some governments in directions desired by other governments. These persons kill on behalf of moral preferences and political goals, and draw their inspiration and sustenance from states that represent those preferences and goals. This was the case with Soviet-era terrorism. In Czechoslovakia and Bulgaria, the Soviet Union trained terrorists from Germany, Italy, Latin America, Turkey, and the Middle East and smuggled them to the West through East Germany, allowing them to strike the Soviets' enemies. So also Islamic terrorists come from Muslim countries and strike on behalf of causes those countries espouse. As the *New York Times*'s Thomas Friedman has written, "98 percent of terrorism is what states want to happen or let happen."

Therefore, students as well as statesmen would do well to realize that the intellectual path to one's preferred peace is no less rigorous in contemporary circumstances than it ever was; the portal to that peace is a physical and moral victory over the obstacles thereto.

CONTEMPORARY GEOPOLITICS

❦

Equipped with knowledge of the world's diverse peoples and regimes, and familiar with the international system and the tools of statecraft, the student can now make sense of contemporary issues among the major powers in each of the world's regions.

The Center

Let us begin, as Mackinder did, with Russia—the world's largest country, which spans the Eurasian continent from the Atlantic to the Pacific, and whose influence reaches toward the Indian Ocean. The Soviet regime (1917–91) left the Russian people dispirited, declining in number, saddled with bad habits, and less and less willing to be marshaled for enterprises abroad. Moreover, Russia's economy—dependent on energy exports and unfriendly to genuine productivity, much like Middle Eastern economies—limits its government's capacity to do big things. The defection of Ukraine, the Baltic states, and Georgia from what had been the Soviet empire reduces Russia to just another European power. Nevertheless, the Russian leadership's neo-Soviet orientation reinforces traditional Russian claims of hegemony over its lost empire. The Soviet autopilot leads Russia to measure success in terms of power vis-à-vis the United States. Hence, twenty-first-century Russia—without Communism's ideological rationale—builds nuclear-tipped missiles aimed at the United States and makes common cause with America's enemies from Venezuela and Cuba to Iran.

Typical of contemporary Russian foreign policy was Russia's 2008 invasion of Georgia. This secured to Russia an important base on the Black Sea and a foothold south of the Caucasus. By briefly occupying the route of international pipelines that would bring natural gas from the "Stans" of central Asia to Europe—bypassing Russia and its anti-Western associate, Iran—the Russian invasion discouraged building it. Above all, the successful invasion showed Ukraine and other neighbors that when Russian diplomats make demands, they had better comply. Notably, the soldiers who took part in the invasion were told that they were actually working against American interests.

Russia's influence on its eastern frontier differs substantially from the Soviet Union's, largely because of China's rise as Asia's largest and most diversified economy. As early as the 1960s, China's ambitions led it to clash with the Soviets, who stationed fifty-three nuclear-armed army divisions on the Chinese border.

In 1969, this military confrontation led China to seek U.S. nuclear protection. In our time, Russia sells its most sophisticated weaponry to China, hoping to divert China's ambition to the western Pacific and to confrontation with the United States. Herman Pirchner's *Reviving Greater Russia?* (2004) is the most concise account of this reabsorption.

EAST ASIA

Japan became East Asia's dominant power after its 1905 victory over Russia in the Russo-Japanese War, and after the 1921 Washington Conference treaties, under which the United States pledged not to fortify Guam and the Philippines. Japan sought China as the primary prize, closely followed by Indonesia's oil fields and Singapore's straits, Asia's gateway to Europe. Throughout the nineteenth century, Britain had taken Singapore and Hong Kong, Holland had taken Indonesia, and Russia had taken most of China's Manchurian North, and each had carved out special commercial deals. Between 1930 and 1941, however, Japan took Korea and Manchuria outright, invaded China, and established the memorably cruel "Greater East Asian Co-Prosperity Sphere." By 1942, Japan dominated East Asia from Singapore to Siberia.

Since Japan's defeat in 1945, however, the U.S. Navy has been the mistress of the western Pacific, controller of the air over East Asia's coasts, and the protectress of islands from Japan to Singapore and Taiwan. This has given the region three generations of peace. Soviet Russia's brief challenge to this order near the end of the Cold War was based on an inferior navy and ran up against the fact that Japan and China, each for its own reasons, preferred the hegemony of faraway America to that of nearby Russia. East Asia's islands, too, given their loathsome experience with Japan and their sensitivity to China's very size, have preferred *Pax Americana* to the alternatives.

In our time, however, China's rise and America's decline have set in motion the passing of East Asia's order. Out of the direst poverty, North Korea, with China's sustenance, built nuclear weapons and fired ballistic missiles over Japan. Its condemnation of South Korea's democratic regime for not being anti-Japanese plays well among all Koreans. China's long-term goal is a united Korea, allied with itself rather than with Japan. China has also openly built up its capacity to control the seas near Taiwan, and to bombard it with ballistic missiles. Japan's nightmare is Chinese power to the north and south, Chinese power over its sea lanes, and a Chinese or Korean attack with nuclear weapons. As this century's first decade passed, Japan asked the U.S. government what it was prepared to do to maintain the current order. Answers that consisted increasingly of faith in China's stability and goodwill have reassured Japan less and less, leading it to look more and more to its own resources. The rest of East Asia is not happy with the prospect of a Sino-Japanese contest for hegemony.

A volume edited by India's Lawrence Prabhakar, *The Evolving Maritime Balance of Power in the Asia-Pacific* (2006), explains how the protagonists' naval strategies and options will affect the region. A useful, short volume is *Japan's Re-emergence as a "Normal" Military Power* (2006), by Christopher Hughes.

SOUTH ASIA

Britain's 1947 departure from India enabled its Hindu and Muslim populations to vent their hatred for each other. Some one million people perished as Muslims either fled or were pushed into the subcontinent's northwestern and northeastern corners (West and East Pakistan, respectively). Through most of the Cold War, India, though nominally nonaligned, allied with the Soviet Union. But it was hobbled by the direst poverty and a caste society anchored by a bureaucratic ruling class. Meanwhile, Pakistan, allied with the West, was run by its British-trained army. Remarkably, throughout sixty years of developments, both India and Pakistan have focused on animosity toward each other.

In our time, however, new developments in each country are shifting that focus. Since India's ruling class lost its affection for socialism and its bureaucracy lifted its heavy hand somewhat, millions of Indians have joined the world economy, many at the bottom in the recycling industry, others in the middle in international English-language call centers, and not a few at the top as state-of-the-art engineers and doctors. In 1997, India developed nuclear weapons and ballistic missiles without significant foreign help. Moreover, India realized that its bigger long-term problem was that the larger Muslim world's radicalization would threaten it internally (India has 150 million Muslims, making it the world's second-largest Muslim country) as well as externally. Foreign investment is taking advantage of India's well-educated population. Indian foreign policy has gravitated toward the United States as a market, as a source of investment, and as the power most likely to fight Islamic terrorism. Unfortunately, many Indians identify Islamic terrorism with Pakistan.

Pakistan, for which Islam is the raison d'être, has become something like the eastern landfall for the storms ravaging the Muslim world. Although its political relations have been with America and Britain from the first and its military and diplomatic cultures are Western, Pakistani society has long been fertile recruiting ground for Wahhabis from Saudi Arabia. Along with money—scarce in this poor country—the Wahhabis have brought schools that teach Islamic purity and hostility to Western things, and have sponsored one of the country's major parties, the Pakistan Muslim League. This has caused the growth of an Islamist subculture, generating pressure for the Pakistani government to adopt Sharia law and conduct a "Muslim foreign policy." Pakistan's ruling class, including the military, is increasingly forced either to compromise with that subculture or to make war on it.

Neither an Islamist Pakistan nor one at war with a substantial part of its own population bodes well for Pakistanis or anyone else. Pakistanis are hard working and talented. They developed nuclear weapons largely on their own. Pakistani doctors work in American and European hospitals. Pakistan could arrange its internal affairs so as to contribute to the Indian subcontinent's prosperity and stability. Were it to orient itself to the Middle East, however, it would use its weapons and its talents for destructive purposes. Yasmin Khan's *The Great Partition* (2007) tells the story of the terrible birth that haunts both India and Pakistan to this day. *India and Pakistan: The First Fifty Years* (1998), edited by Selig Harrison, Paul Kreisberg, and Dennis Kux, is the standard history.

The Middle East

Iran is an anomaly in the Middle East. Most Iranians, as Persians and Shia Muslims, look upon their Arab Sunni neighbors with resentment, fear, and contempt—resentment for centuries of oppression of Shia by Sunni; fear because Iran is the only country in which the Shia rule (Iraq as a whole has a Shia majority, but its Kurdish part is functionally independent, and the writ of Baghdad's Shia government does not run in Sunni regions); and contempt because Persians generally regard Arabs as lower beings. Because Iran's Persian identity and its Muslim faith have never fully reconciled, Iranian politics has oscillated between the two. The most recent of those pendular swings was the revolution of 1979 that overthrew a shah—who had stressed Persianness along with modernization—and produced the Islamic Republic. Iran's current international and domestic personalities result from the interaction among several disparate revolutionary elements.

The Ayatollah Ruhollah Khomeini led the revolutionary coalition of 1979 in the name of Shia Islam's most learned clerics—conservative, aristocratic figures not very interested in politics. But the revolution succeeded thanks to the organizational talent of lesser clerics who brought in armed help from the Palestine Liberation Organization (PLO) as well as financial, logistic, and diplomatic support from the Soviet Union. This, rather than anything in Shia theology, explains why the Islamic Republic has been run by those secularized clerics whose satan is America. It also explains Iran's continuing special relationship with Russia, especially on energy matters and Iran's championing of Arab causes against the West.

Nevertheless, day-to-day Iranian foreign policy may be best understood as its Arab neighbors understand it: an attempt to increase its own power and thereby leverage the status of Shia populations throughout the Muslim world. This certainly has been Iran's policy toward Iraq, where three out of four Arabs are Shia. Iran's rise has emboldened the Shia minorities in Saudi Arabia and the Gulf states (in Qatar an oppressed majority). In Lebanon and Palestine, Iranian money and arms have created and captured Hezbollah and Hamas, respectively, which groups contend for power against other local factions on their own and on Iran's behalf. All Arab governments fear that Iran's development of nuclear weapons will cover Iran's subversion of their regimes. Hence, they insist, quietly but persistently, that the United States somehow prevent Iran from obtaining these weapons.

Saudi Arabia's Al Saud family rules the kingdom as protectors of Islam's holiest sites in Mecca and Medina. The Wahhabi sect bolsters the Saudi monarchy's claim to divine authority. The country's educational system and media instill Wahhabi purity and disdain for lesser Muslims such as Shia and for infidels. But behind palace walls and abroad, the royal family and its wealthy hangers-on live un-Islamic lives. Saudi society is based on tribes, some of which (the Sunni Hashemites in the west as well as the Shia tribes in the east) regard the Saudis as enemies. Saudi society does not produce enough to feed or otherwise support itself. Rather, it pays for everything with billions of dollars from oil extracted by Western engineers with labor from the Indian subcontinent. Its armed forces, lavishly equipped by the United States, are of questionable competence and uncertain loyalty.

Though otherwise weak and vulnerable, the royal family and its hangers-on dispose of lots of money. Thus Saudi policy, at home and abroad, may be reduced to a single word: pay. The Saudis deal with the conflict between Wahhabi rigor and their dissolute lives by subsidizing the spread of Wahhabism abroad. One consequence is that a majority of the mosques built throughout the world are paid for by Saudi charities. A related consequence is that, in places from Indonesia to Pakistan to Nigeria, millions of Muslim children attend Saudi-financed madrassas (schools), where Wahhabism is the only subject.

In 1990–91, the United States destroyed the Iraqi forces that were threatening the Saudi kingdom. Indeed, the United States has been Saudi Arabia's guarantor since Britain withdrew from responsibilities "east of Suez" in 1957. Saudi Arabia has also managed to make its relationship with the United States central to its influence in the region. This is the result of the royal family's long-term financial cultivation of diplomats who have served in the kingdom, as well as of Saudi power over the profits of American oil executives and contractors.

Syria is a military dictatorship based on the secular Ba'ath Party and on the Alewite sect, which many Muslims consider heretical. Short on legitimacy, the Assad family has ruled with deadly rigor since 1970. As a poor country, Syria has followed a foreign policy of acting as the junior partner of richer and more powerful countries. Until 1990, Syria was the Soviet Union's bastion in the Middle East (along with Iraq) and the prime destination for its most advanced armament, paid for by Saudi money. After that, Syria largely became an arm of Iranian policy—especially in Lebanon, where Syria ran the Shia-based Hezbollah on Iran's behalf. In the process,

Syria established violent suzerainty over Lebanon. Syria's conventional military ventures against Israel in 1967 and 1973 ended in debacles and the loss of the Golan Heights. Despite an impressive arsenal of weapons, including Soviet SS21 missiles capable of striking Israel, Syria wields international influence largely through the terrorists who either have their headquarters in Damascus or marshal and regroup their forces in Syria.

Egypt, home to some seventy-six million people, is the Arab world's largest country, the home of its culture and industry, and the source of its political trends. Egypt's Colonel Gamal Abdul Nasser gave Arab nationalism its first success in 1953 by overthrowing King Faruk, who reigned under British protection. Nasser then nationalized the Suez Canal and began convincing other Arabs to oust Western-sponsored governments and join Egypt in being "nonaligned" on the side of the Soviet Union. When Nasser redefined nationalism in secular, socialist terms, he crushed the Muslim Brotherhood, which had been part of his revolutionary coalition. Upon Nasser's death in 1970, his successors reversed their orientation and sided with the United States against the Soviets. But nothing else changed in Egypt: the country remains economically dysfunctional, corrupt, and dictatorial. More than ever, its main political divide is between the rulers' retinue and the Muslim Brotherhood.

Egypt is the birthplace of modern political Islam, or Islamism: there Hassan al-Banna founded the Muslim Brotherhood in 1928, and Sayyid Qutb wrote the Brotherhood's most compelling books in the 1950s and '60s. These works argued on the basis of both the Koran and experience that Western ways, and the Arabs who imitate them, are to be opposed by *jihad*. To say that Egypt's regime holds off Islamism at bayonet point understates the case: Nasser ordered Qutb hanged in 1966 as a threat to his power, and Nasser's successors regard Islamism as their main enemy. It remains true, however, that the regime presides over a cultural wasteland (as well as an economic and social one) that makes Islamism attractive.

Egypt is hostage to Islamism's growing attractiveness. Though its government depends on some $2 billion per year in U.S. aid, the country's increasingly Islamist public opinion leads the government openly to oppose U.S. policy even when it supports it secretly. Though officially at peace with Israel, Egypt lets arms and terrorists pass through its territory on their way to attack that country. The end result in Egypt and in the rest of the Arab world are populations with Islamist mentalities that will overthrow their countries' regimes someday, but that now respond to hopelessness and misery by migrating to Europe to taste the good life and work out their resentments.

Israel is a bigger international issue than it is a country. Finding it on the map is hard. Seven and a half million mostly Jewish people are squeezed into eight and a half thousand square miles. But they produce a GDP of more than $200 billion and a per-capita income three times that of neighboring countries, whose populations number over 300 million. All its Arab neighbors except Egypt and Jordan are officially at war with Israel and continue to work for its destruction because they never accepted the existence of the Jewish state. Since 1947, the Arab world has started four major wars against Israel, as well as sent countless terrorists to kill Israelis. Nevertheless, Israel flourishes. Israel is an international issue because the Arab world pressures Europe and America, through oil embargoes and terrorism, to pressure Israel to give in to its demands. Brokering peace between Israel and its neighbors has been a perennial goal of American statesmen. Yet it is by no means clear that such a settlement—or even Israel's disappearance from the map—would change the character of the Arab world or improve its disposition toward America and Europe.

EUROPE

Whereas until the mid-twentieth century Europe was the international system's center and driving force, contemporary Europe is peripheral to events that originate elsewhere. During the Cold War, none of Europe's formerly great powers were protagonists. Rather, they were satellites of either Russia or America, and the prizes of the struggle. Some believed that following the Soviet empire's internal collapse, Germany's reunification, and eastern Europe's return to freedom, the European Union would gather the energies of some 360 million educated people and play an active role in world events. Europe's role has been passive, however, because its aging, shrinking population and official culture are averse to anything else. No one expects that Europe, or any part thereof, will take decisive action to force any international outcome.

Nevertheless, Europeans must decide how to deal with a truculent Russia that is tightening its grip on its energy supplies, and with the in-migration of some sixteen million Muslim Middle Easterners and North Africans, who now make up a fast-growing 5 percent of its population. These are not immigrants who prefer the ways of their new home to those of the countries they left and intend to assimilate, but rather they are persons who forcefully preserve and expand their own ways at the expense of a host civilization they consider inferior to their own. They have brought the Middle East's causes and quarrels to Europe. (See Jytte Klausen's *The Islamic Challenge: Politics and Religion in Western Europe.*) A few of them practice terrorism on behalf of their causes, and many more approve of the practice. Since the Muslim world's quarrels and Europe's Muslim population continue to grow, the European Union's fifteen members know they have a problem.

Poland and the Czech Republic, supported by the rest of the former Soviet empire and followed sometimes by Italy and Portugal, take what might be called a harder line against Russian pressure and Muslim migration, while Germany and France, followed by other western European countries, take a softer one. Great Britain supports now one, now the other. Lacking unanimity, each country has followed its own predilections. While all Europeans worry about Russia, Germany has led France and northern Europe in general to overlook Russia's tightening grip on the Ukraine's gas pipelines and destabilization of its politics. Heeding Russian objections, this group has blocked the accession of former Soviet satellites into the defensive North Atlantic Treaty Organization (NATO), and urged the United States not to build even token missile defense installations in Poland and the Czech Republic. Most European countries officially believe that U.S. support for Israel against the Muslim world adds to their troubles, if not that it is a main cause of those troubles.

All this is to say that much of Europe's foreign policy in our time—outside of its attempt to maintain as strict a regime of economic protectionism as it can and beyond its promotion of humanitarian activities—consists of leveraging the policies of the United States, primarily toward the Muslim world and Russia, as well as backseat driving on countless other matters of U.S. policy.

The Americas

Brazil, so goes the quip, has always been the country of the future, and always will be. Argentina, another South American country almost as richly endowed with natural resources, was among the world's wealthiest countries until nearly our time. Other Latin American countries (Haiti, Bolivia, and the Dominican Republic) have neither an attractive past nor fine future prospects. All have histories of appalling government. Internal strife driven by socioeconomic factors has been their preoccupation. Some of the wars among them have been for important stakes: in the 1880s, Chile won a victory over Peru for mastery of South America's Pacific coast; in 1935, Bolivia and Paraguay bloodied each other over the Gran Chaco. Other wars, like the 1969 miniwar between Honduras and El Salvador over a soccer match, were for pride.

Once Latin America detached itself from Spain, it gravitated economically toward Great Britain, the nineteenth-century world's greatest source of capital and manufactured goods, and politically toward the United States, whose republican model of government most Latins tried to imitate. Many looked to the United States as some sort of guarantor against Europe. For Mexico and the countries of the Caribbean, which had lost territory to the United States, relations with the colossus of the North soon became of primordial importance. Through the twentieth century, as the U.S. economy outshone that of Britain, American universities drew the region's elite students, and the United States organized the region's countries into the Organization of American States (OAS), a system for mutual assistance and peaceful resolution of disputes. Ronaldo Munck's *Contemporary Latin America* (2007) brings the student up to date.

Nevertheless, there has never been a lack of Old World governments that have sought, and found, allies in the New World for the purpose of countering the

United States. In 1916–17, Germany romanced Mexico with the prospect of an alliance against the United States that would yield the return of lands lost in 1848 after the Mexican-American War; in this way, the United States was propelled into World War I. During the Cold War, the Soviet Union sponsored the Cuban regime of Fidel Castro in order to establish important military bases and encourage other Latin Americans to join its worldwide anti-U.S. coalition. In our time, both Iran and Russia work with Venezuela's anti-U.S. regime, as well as with Cuba, less because of any inherent interest in the Western hemisphere than because of a desire to counter the United States.

In sum, though the happiness of Latin America's peoples depends on how they deal with the demons that have ever bedeviled them, their role in the world depends on whether countries in the region decide to tie their fortunes to the United States or choose to align with other states against America.

WHAT IS ALL THIS TO AMERICA—
AND TO THE STUDENT OF IR?

❧

Every student of IR hears that rapid travel and instant communication make events in the rest of the world crucial to our safety and prosperity. But America's relations with other countries have always been crucial. The American colonists lived or died by trade and were beset on all sides by empires based in London, Paris, Madrid, or St. Petersburg. As the U.S. economy developed, it became more dependent on international financing, and more sensitive to world economic conditions. In the eighteenth and nineteenth centuries no less than in the twenty-first, Americans have mingled with every continent's peoples and cultures. *Now, as in centuries past, the extent, speed, and ease of America's foreign relations is far less important than their purpose:* Why, and to achieve what, do we relate to whom? From what perspective should we approach international relations?

One of George Washington's main objectives was to induce the American people to think of themselves less as part of the outside world's struggles and more as Americans with distinct character and interests. The founding generation's approach to world affairs, as John Quincy Adams explained in 1823, amounted to seeking the widest-possible reciprocal commercial relations with other peoples, avoiding their quarrels, respecting them, while demanding respect for ourselves. By fighting only battles truly our own, Americans could remain mankind's "city on a hill." Only in the Progressive Era that straddled 1900 did the idea arise that this city, now grown great, might come down from its hill to settle mankind's quarrels and reform its ways. In the mid-twentieth century the idea began to grow that, rather than *reforming* others, Americans should *conform* themselves to the rest of the world's standards. By the turn of the twenty-first century, the U.S. government was involved in every corner of the globe for reasons not self-evidently compelling, and often contradictory.

Discerning America's causes and battles from those of other peoples is intellectually demanding and politically perilous. Because Americans differ over the extent of our interests in this or that region as well as in their preferences for what should happen in these disputed regions, foreign affairs have heightened *domestic, American* political quarrels. Hence, George Washington's objective of focusing American minds on interests self-evidently American, pursued with cold reason and iron will, is as vitally important in the twenty-first century's first decades as it was in the eighteenth century's last.

RECOMMENDED READING

۶

INFLUENCES ON THE FOUNDERS

Thucydides, *The History of the Peloponnesian War*
Plutarch, *Lives*
Livy, *The History of Rome*
Tacitus, *The Annals of Imperial Rome*
Viscount Bolingbroke, *Patriot King* (1738)
Emmerich de Vattel, *The Law of Nations or the Principles of Natural Law* (1758)

EARLY AMERICAN STATECRAFT

George Washington, Farewell Address (1796)
John Quincy Adams, Address to the U.S. House of Representatives (July 4, 1821)
Robert A. Taft, *A Foreign Policy for Americans* (1951)

LIBERAL INTERNATIONALISM

Nicholas Murray Butler, *The International Mind: An Argument for the Judicial Settlement of International Disputes* (1912)

David Starr Jordan, *World Peace and the College Man* (1916); *Ways to Lasting Peace* (1916)

Henry L. Stimson, *On Active Service in Peace and War* (1948)

Anthony Lake, *Legacy of Vietnam: The War, American Society, and the Future of U.S. Foreign Policy* (1976)

Arthur Schlesinger Jr., "Back to the Womb?" *Foreign Affairs* (1995)

Realism

Hans Morgenthau, *Politics Among Nations* (1948)

George F. Kennan, *American Diplomacy 1900–1950* (1951)

Robert Osgood, *Limited War: The Challenge to American Strategy* (1957)

Henry Kissinger, *Nuclear Weapons and Foreign Policy* (1957)

Thomas Schelling, *The Strategy of Conflict* (1960)

Henry Kissinger, *Diplomacy* (1994)

Neoconservatism

Joshua Muravchik, *Exporting Democracy: Fulfilling America's Destiny* (1991); *The Imperative of American Leadership* (1996)

President George W. Bush, 2005 inaugural address

Robert Kagan, *Dangerous Nation* (2006)

The United States

Walter McDougall, *Freedom Just Around the Corner* (2004); *Throes of Democracy* (2008)

Samuel P. Huntington, *Who Are We?* (2005)

CENTRAL ASIA

Rene Grousset, *Empire of the Steppes* (1970)
Ted Rall, *Silk Road to Ruin* (2006)

CAUCASUS

Vicken Chetarian, *War and Peace in the Caucasus* (2008)

RUSSIA

Astolphe de Custine, *Journey for Our Time* (1839)
Herman Pirchner, *Reviving Greater Russia?* (2004)

MIDDLE EAST

Gerald H. Blake and Alasdair Drysdale, *The Middle East and North Africa: A Political Geography* (1985)
Bernard Lewis, *The Shaping of the Modern Middle East* (1994)

AFRICA

Peter Duignan and Lewis Gann, *Africa: The Land and the People* (1972)
Peter Duignan and Lewis Gann, *Hope for South Africa?* (1991)
Paul Henze, *Layers of Time: A History of Ethiopia* (2004)

INDIAN SUBCONTINENT

Winston Churchill, *The Story of the Malakand Field Force* (1898)
O. H. K. Spate, *India and Pakistan: A General and Regional Geography* (1954)

Selig Harrison, Paul Kreisberg, and Dennis Kux, eds., *India and Pakistan: The First Fifty Years* (1998)

Yasmin Khan, *The Great Partition* (2007)

China

Vincent Cronin, *Wise Man from the West* (1955)

Julie Lee Wei, Ramon H. Myers, and Donald G. Gillin, eds., *Prescriptions for Saving China: Selected Writings of Sun Yat-sen* (1994)

Jonathan Fenby, *Chiang Kai-shek* (2004)

Lawrence Prabhakar, *The Evolving Maritime Balance of Power in the Asia-Pacific* (2006)

Japan

Robert C. Christopher, *The Japanese Mind* (1983)

Christopher Hughes, *Japan's Re-emergence as a "Normal" Military Power* (2006)

Australia

Dennis Rumley, *The Geopolitics of Australia's Regional Relations* (1999)

Europe

Peter Duignan and Lewis Gann, *The Rebirth of the West* (1992)

Jytte Klausen, *The Islamic Challenge: Politics and Religion in Western Europe* (2005)

Bruce Thornton, *Decline and Fall: Europe's Slow-Motion Suicide* (2007)

Walter Laqueur, *The Last Days of Europe* (2009)

LATIN AMERICA

Ronaldo Munck, *Contemporary Latin America* (2007)

WORLD CULTURE

Sir Halford Mackinder, *Democratic Ideals and Reality* (1919)

Norman Cohn, *The Pursuit of the Millennium* (1957)

Adda Bozeman, *Politics and Culture in International History: From the Ancient Near East to the Opening of the Modern Age* (1960)

Samuel P. Huntington, *The Clash of Civilizations and the Remaking of World Order* (1996)

THE NATURE OF REGIMES

Karl Wittfogel, *Oriental Despotism* (1957)

Angelo Codevilla, *The Character of Nations: How Politics Makes and Breaks Prosperity, Family, and Civility* (2009)

NON-WESTERN STATECRAFT IN THE ANCIENT WORLD

Shahnameh, Book of Kings (Persia)

Arthasastra (India)

Sun Tzu, *The Art of War* (China)

DIPLOMACY

Machiavelli, *Discourses* (1531); *The Prince* (1532)

Jean Bodin, *Six Books of the Republic* (1576)

Thomas Hobbes, *Leviathan* (1651)

Garrett Mattingly, *Renaissance Diplomacy* (1955)

Fred C. Iklé, *How Nations Negotiate* (1968)
David Baldwin, *Economic Statecraft* (1985)
Joseph Nye, *Soft Power* (1990)

Commentaries on the International System

Hugo Grotius, *De Jure Belli ac Pacis* (1625)
Emmerich de Vattel, *The Law of Nations or the Principles of Natural Law* (1758)

United Nations

Robert Murphy, *Diplomat Among Warriors* (1964)
Dean Acheson, *Present at the Creation* (1969)
Daniel Patrick Moynihan, *A Dangerous Place* (1978)
Brett D. Schaefer, ed., *ConUNdrum: The Limits of the United Nations and the Search for Alternatives* (2009)

International History

Paul Johnson, *Modern Times* (1983)

War

Carl von Clausewitz, *On War* (1832)
Norman Angell, *The Great Illusion* (1910)
Martin van Creveld, *The Transformation of War* (1991)
Donald Kagan, *On the Origins of War and the Preservation of Peace* (1995)
Angelo Codevilla and Paul Seabury, *War: Ends and Means* (second edition, 2006)
Angelo Codevilla, *Advice to War Presidents* (2009)

LITERATURE

Charles Hill, *Grand Strategies: Literature, Statecraft, and World Order* (2010)